Report Writing

Report Writing

Second Edition

JOAN VAN EMDEN
AND
JENNIFER EASTEAL

McGRAW-HILL BOOK COMPANY

London · New York · St Louis · San Francisco · Auckland
Bogotá · Caracas · Hamburg · Lisbon · Madrid · Mexico · Milan
Montreal · New Delhi · Panama · Paris · San Juan · São Paulo
Singapore · Sydney · Tokyo · Toronto

Published by
McGRAW-HILL Book Company Europe
Shoppenhangers Road, Maidenhead, Berkshire SL6 2QL, England
Telephone: 0628 23432   Fax: 0628 770224

British Library Cataloguing in Publication Data

Emden, Joan Van
  Report Writing. – 2 Rev. ed
  I. Title II. Easteal, Jennifer
  808.066
  ISBN 0-07-707606-0

Library of Congress Cataloging-in-Publication Data

Van Emden, Joan.
  Report writing / Joan van Emden and Jennifer Easteal. – 2nd ed.
    p.   cm.
  Includes bibliographical references
  ISBN 0-07-707606-0
  1. English language – Rhetoric. 2. Report writing.
  I. Easteal, Jennifer. II. Title.
PE1478.V28   1992
808'.042 – dc20   93-2659 CIP

12345 CUP 96543

Typeset by Computape (Pickering) Ltd, North Yorkshire
and printed and bound in Great Britain at the University Press, Cambridge

Contents

vi *Contents*

Preface

If a report does not attract the reader, it will not be effective. An individual or a company may produce excellent, original work, but if the presentation, writing and layout of the report do not equal the quality of the content, reader goodwill is lost, and the report itself may be ignored or its author's technical competence, often unjustly, called into question.

We have for several years been aware of the shortage of suitable texts on the subject. The Institution of Electrical Engineers commissioned us to write their Professional Brief on *Technical Report Writing*, and the demand for copies when it was published encouraged us in writing this book, covering the subject more widely. The quotations and examples are almost all 'real-life', and we are grateful to the many companies and organizations, necessarily anonymous, who have allowed us to use their material in this way. Other lecturers in Management and Business Studies commented on the need for a suitable textbook, and we hope that they too, and everyone, who has to write reports in the course of their work, will find this book helpful and stimulating.

Preface to the Second Edition

In the five years since *Report Writing* was first published, technology has advanced and management practice has changed—most report writers, for instance, now wordprocess their own material. Computing facilities have reduced many of the chores of producing reports, but the writer is still in control, making creative decisions and implanting into the document a personal style and experience.

The text of *Report Writing* has been updated in line with these changes, and a second specimen report, based on technical material, has been added. The emphasis is still on good practice, with examples to clarify each stage of report production; the need for such guidance seems to be as widespread now as it was five years ago.

Joan van Emden
Reading

Jennifer Easteal
Salisbury
1993

Acknowledgements

Joan van Emden and Jennifer Easteal are grateful for the cooperation of a wide range of companies and organizations who have asked to remain anonymous but who kindly supplied examples, and to all the course delegates and students on whom we have tried out our ideas and our material. Any factual errors which remain are our own. We also thank Ann Redfern, Lorraine Standing and Judi Upton-Ward for their careful preparation of the typescript.

Acknowledgement is also made to: The Royal Institution of Chartered Surveyors for permission to quote from the report, *Life Cycle Costing for Construction*; The Motor Industry Information Service of the Society of Motor Manufacturers and Traders, for permission to use their statistics.

CHAPTER 1

Report production: making decisions

Types of report · Readers and users · Identifying the reader · Tone · Company requirements

'All the world's a stage', remarked Jaques in *As You Like It*, and after that lively and attractive introduction to his subject, he outlined with commendable clarity the seven parts played by each individual actor, concluding with the even more memorable (if slightly melancholy) lines about second childhood, dentures and bifocals. His, or rather Shakespeare's, reporting technique is brilliant: the introduction, the logical progression, the strong conclusion. Whatever the form of report we shall discuss in this book, that pattern should be followed. Shakespeare also wrote for his audience, knowing what they would expect, accept, and be excited by: this too is a rule of good report writing. As we have written elsewhere[1], the first of such rules is:

> The reader is the most important person.

So the craft of producing a good report demands two particular skills: getting to know the reader, and organizing the information. It no doubt also helps if the writer is a genius, but geniuses are rare in the field of report writing, and much will be forgiven the writer who abides by these two criteria.

Types of report

The simplest form of report is a memo, which may even be hand-written. It is the least formal, shortest report, usually written from one colleague to another. For instance, Alan goes to a meeting at which he picks up a piece of information which might be useful to Jim, who is away on holiday. Sensibly realizing that by the time Jim comes back, he, Alan, will probably have forgotten all about the incident, he writes a memo on the company memo paper, with its printed heading of To, From, Date and Subject. Alan knows his reader (it's Jim, who has worked in the same building for the last five years; they sometimes have a pint together in the pub after work), and he knows that Jim will be interested in what he has to say. So he organizes his material. Remembering his Shakespeare, he starts with an introduction ('You remember that paper by Joe Bloggs you said was useful for the Zeugma Project? I met Joe Bloggs at the conference in Edinburgh a few days ago . . . '). Having attracted Jim's attention, Alan gives him the useful information in a logical form ('He says he's got another paper on the same topic coming out in a few weeks' time, and he'll send you an offprint. If you're going to the European conference in Brussels in July, he would like to meet you there and have a chat'). The conclusion is short, to the point and friendly. ('I hope this is useful. See you next week.') The memo is a report, for Jim's benefit, on a small piece of information discovered by Alan. It is sensibly constructed in three short paragraphs (the final one being only two brief sentences), and it is written in an informal style (it will be dated, as all reports should be, but probably just signed 'Alan').

This is an extreme example of a report, indeed, it is only just worth calling a report. At the other extreme, there is the kind of report produced by international agencies, perhaps by a body of the United Nations, in 15 leather-bound volumes, beautifully printed with coloured maps and expensively produced diagrams, and with a Volume 16 which is (mercifully) a Summary. The organization responsible for such a report has also considered its readership, which may be worldwide and using English only as a common language. It has also organized vast amounts of abstruse material into a complex (but not over-complicated) and logical system, and its style is very formal. Reports, with the single exception of the little memo-report, are formal documents, and their organization (Chapter 3) and language (Chapter 4) must reflect this formality.

In between these extremes is a wide range of reports, including laboratory reports, accident reports, progress reports, final advisory reports, and visit reports (the kind of report which might be produced by an engineer after a site visit abroad to investigate local problems in the use of machinery supplied by the company). Each type of report presents its own challenge, but all must adhere to the principles outlined at the start of the chapter: *the needs of the reader are all-important*, and *the material must be clearly and logically organized*. Later in this book, report structure will be discussed and guidelines for differing formats will be suggested. In the remainder of this chapter, we will look at the identification of the reader's needs and at the decisions which have to be made within the report writer's own organization.

Readers and users

Report readers are few in number; report users are numerous. As most report writers are also report users, it is perhaps surprising that this distinction is so often overlooked. The report reader starts at the beginning of the report, works through it to the end, and then probably turns into a report user. The more frequently-met user looks at the beginning of the report and reads a few pages, turns to the end of the report and reads a bit more, and then goes to the contents list to choose which sections to read in detail. The sections chosen may not be read in order, and some of the report may not be read at all. In making a decision, the reader will be guided by what is useful or needed most urgently, and the writer must therefore make sure that attention is drawn to the most important information: the conclusions and/or recommendations, given in brief at the beginning and in detail towards the end, and particular sections which can be identified easily by the individual reader. Such sections must not only be identifiable, but also logically placed so that the overall pattern of the report is clear.

Identifying the reader

The writer of reports must, then, identify the readership: sometimes the identification is obvious (a more senior officer within the organization); sometimes the representative of a client company (identifiable but not personally known); sometimes, and frighteningly, a range of people (some technically qualified and some not). All of these may have to take decisions on the basis of the information in the report.

While there can be no absolute rules about how much to find out, the writer should make every attempt to discover who the *principal* reader is (often, the one who controls expenditure), what the technical expertise might be and how it differs from the writer's own, what level of technical language is acceptable, and what other expertise will be available. It is also important to know what the reader's interest is: is he or she being asked to spend money, sign a contract, agree to further investigation, accept that the machinery is tested to approved standards of safety? What does the reader want to know, and what will be done with the information? Any other details which might help the writer, for instance whether the two companies, the writer's and the reader's, have worked together successfully in the past, or whether English is the reader's usual working language, should be noted and remembered throughout the production of the report. All such information will be helpful in getting the tone right.

Tone

'Tone' is difficult to define, but it is the 'getting it right for the reader' aspect of report production which is all-important. It includes understanding of the reader's point of view, the logical organization of material, clear and accurate writing, helpful and well-produced diagrams and a contents list which will guide the report user to the most important information. Less obviously, it also includes choosing a binding which will allow diagrams to lie flat, and which will not disintegrate if the report is handled frequently. A type size which is easy to read and not too small (10 point rather than 8 point), paper which will stand up to heavy use (grease-resistant if it is to be used in workshops), a cover which attracts attention without being garish (perhaps using the company colour) all help to make good 'tone'. The reader should *want* to use the report because it looks attractive, and should be encouraged to read on because the physical reading is made as easy as possible. It is surprising how often potential readers are put off by unnumbered pages crowded with small print. If the report is expensive to produce and influential in content, it is often worth employing a consultant designer to present the material effectively and to ensure its maximum impact.

Company requirements

Knowing the reader is important; understanding the writer's own organization is also helpful. Decisions have to be made which may militate against much good advice given in this book: time is frequently short so that checking is inadequate, or senior staff may take control and change the emphasis of a report written by a more junior employee who may nevertheless know more about the particular problem, or the individual reader, than senior managers do. The writer must beware the pitfalls within the company, one of which can be a conflict within the terms of reference for a report. Different senior staff want different documents: a briefing document to be used at a meeting, a formal report which can be shown to a client, a specification or manual which could be back-up to other information. The junior report writer must, even at the cost of being temporarily unpopular, establish what sort of document is required and what its use will be. Lack of clear guidance may lead to a report which attempts to do different and even conflicting jobs, and the resulting confusion can lead to the temporary unpopularity becoming permanent.

Time available for the draft version and for the final stage on the word processor should both be made clear to the writer: it can be very frustrating to rush a report through to its apparent completion and then to discover ten days later that the officer responsible for validating it and authorizing distribution hasn't moved it from the in-tray. The appropriate length of the finished document should also be clarified: this may be a 'political' consideration dependent on the cost of the report. The newcomer to an organization needs to ask questions about procedure, restriction, authorization and, most of all, about guidelines. Looking at past reports within the company is helpful, but a set of short, well-illustrated guidelines (sometimes produced as a 'dummy report') showing exactly what the company demands and where flexibility is allowed, should be given to every new employee who is likely to write reports. Attention might also be drawn to the copy of this book in the company library, with a recommendation that the writer uses some of the new salary to purchase a copy. Report writers need all the help they can get!

Key points in Chapter 1

- Remember that the reader is the most important person, and must be clearly identified.

- Your report's structure, style and presentation must all be helpful and attractive to the reader.

- Clarify your terms of reference, and check time available, length of report required, and company guidelines.

CHAPTER 2

Preparation

Objectives · Collecting the facts · Preliminary organization · Spider diagrams · Beginning and ending

Most reports are exercises in persuasion. They exist to sell a product, an idea or a point of view, and, if they are successful, they result in action being taken, whether it is the development of a new project or the introduction of advanced safety procedures. Other reports show how efficiency could be increased or money saved. Apart perhaps from accident reports, which should 'describe what happened' without prejudice, and laboratory reports, which describe the methods used and the results of experiments, most reports are subjective.

This, of course, contradicts the general feeling that reports should look objectively and dispassionately at a problem, and become 'personal' only in making recommendations. Yet in reality, both points of view are true. The facts presented in a report should be exactly that: facts, without bias or comment. Only in the light of such evidence can conclusions be accurately drawn and wise recommendations made. At the same time, no report writer presents every aspect of every piece of information: choices are made in the light of the reader's need and to a certain extent the writer's need too. In being selective in the facts presented, personal decisions are inevitably made, as are subjective judgements in organizing the facts. It is important for report writers to be aware of this, for to acknowledge one's own prejudices or to face the inadequacy of the information available is to take stock of the report potential and to allow for possible weaknesses in report presentation.

Objectives

Nevertheless, the report writer must start from a clear perception of the reader's needs and of the terms of reference. Why should the busy reader want to use or read the report, and what is the likely outcome? The previous chapter has stressed the need to understand as much as possible about the reader's outlook, but it is also important that the writer's own position is borne in mind. What are the objectives; what are the motives for writing the report? Often, the two sets of objectives will complement one another, but it is possible for them to conflict (the writer wants to 'sell'; the reader doesn't want to 'buy'), and it is as well for the writer to understand the problem (and therefore to be as persuasive as possible). There may even be a third objective, confidential to the writer, which is to impress the reader so much that promotion/a bonus/the offer of a better job, will follow. Success comes from a well-focused report based on clearly-defined objectives; writing for everyone and for no specific reason is a waste of time.

A series of questions will help to clarify the objectives and to give a focus to the report:

1. What does the reader know about this subject?

2. What does the reader want to know?

3. What do I want the reader to know about this subject?

4. Is there a discrepancy between (2) and (3), and if so, what is its importance?

5. What action does the reader expect to take as a result of this report?

6. What action do I want the reader to take as a result of this report?

7. Is there a discrepancy between (5) and (6), and if so, what is its importance, to the reader and to me?

8. Why am I (not anybody else) writing this particular report for this particular reader? (This question may well already have been answered, but it may also pinpoint specific requirements.)

When the identity of the reader and the objectives of the report are clear, the report writer needs again to review any special considerations: time has been mentioned; the cost of any investigations may also have to be kept in mind; sometimes confidentiality will be a constant problem, limiting the information sought or included. There may also be reference books which should be available: previous reports, comparative figures, relevant British Standards, company guidelines and, not least, good English and perhaps also technical dictionaries. The writer is now prepared for action, and indeed information may already be arriving on the desk.

Collecting the facts

There can be no set procedure for collecting the facts needed for a report. In some cases, experiments in the laboratory and their measured results will provide enough material for a report; at other times, interviews, site visits, detailed measurements and calculations may be needed to supplement background reading. Whatever the procedure necessary to ascertain the facts, it must be followed as fully as possible, however difficult or unpromising any particular line of enquiry might seem. Within the limits set down in the terms of reference, all the relevant facts must be discovered.

Preliminary organization

The result of such a relentless search is often a heap of material of differing usefulness. Some preliminary sorting out is needed. At an early stage, it is helpful to work on the basis of three categories of information. Category A material is in the mainstream of the report, obviously relevant to the subject and crucial to the report's success; Category B contains material probably useful as back-up, or for some specialized readers, or helpful but not essential to the understanding of the report; Category C is the place for information which has been unearthed during the investigation and which is not uninteresting, but which has dubious relevance to the report as a whole. It would be unwise to jettison the third category at this stage, as subsequent findings might make apparently irrelevant material much more important than at first appears. Flexibility is important, and so information might move between all three categories until it finds the right permanent place. In the end, Category A material will probably become the main body of the report, Category B material might become an appendix or appendices, and Category C will either be put away for another time or fill the wastepaper basket.

When the information for the whole report, or for a major section of it, has been collected, it must be organized. Detailed headings and appropriate notation are discussed later, but the first stages of linking ideas and forming patterns can start, and this valuable preparation should not be rushed or omitted: it will make subsequent work much easier to complete.

One of the most common ways of organizing material is to list ideas on the computer screen and to move them around until the writer is satisfied that the best logical order has been achieved. There is still the inherent problem that the writer tends to see the items at the top of the list as more important than the items below it. In merely listing ideas, an order has been predetermined from which it is difficult to escape.

Spider diagrams

An increasingly popular alternative to the list is the Spider Diagram (which has other names such as Brain Pattern[2]). This method of organizing material is not easy to work with at the first attempt, and we, the authors, would stress that some perseverance is needed (but we found that using the system soon became easier and now we couldn't manage without it!). The process of forming a spider diagram starts with a brainstorming session. One key word, or perhaps key phrase, is written randomly on a large sheet of paper to represent each idea or item to be included in the report. It may be helpful not to use the standard A4 format, but to turn the page through 90° so that the page shape itself is unusual (wide rather than deep) and ruled lines become irrelevant. The main key word, the theme of the whole report, can then be placed in the centre of the page, and other key words radiate from the centre in any direction and with no discernible hierarchy. Each idea is enclosed in its 'bubble', and the 'bubbles' can then be linked by lines as appropriate. A simple example (see Figure 2.1) might produce a checklist for a speaker at a conference, who records in a random fashion the details which must be remembered.

Working from the central 'bubble', 'EDINBURGH THURSDAY', the speaker can organize ideas in three sections, by linking the items which are 'advance preparation' (getting a train timetable, ordering

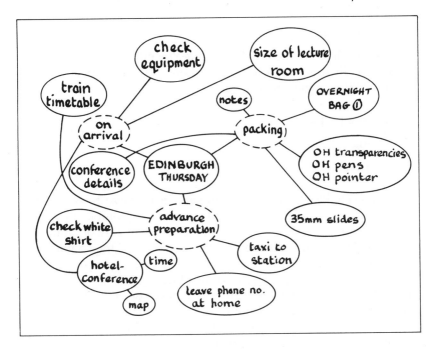

Figure 2.1   *Spider diagram for conference*

the taxi to the station, etc.), those which involve 'packing' (overnight bag and equipment needed for the presentation), and those which will have to be dealt with on arrival, such as finding the way from the hotel to the conference centre and timing the journey. In focusing on each, any 'missing links' will become obvious: the phone number has been left at home, but not with the secretary in case of a work crisis during the conference (or perhaps the omission was deliberate). It is always worth considering whether an apparent missing link is the result of lack of research, unobtainable information, or oversight.

One or two items are probably complicated in themselves, and could be the subject of a separate bubble. So, in the example given, 'overnight bag' is not much help when its owner is packing, but it could be given a number (1 in this instance) and subordinate bubble number 1 will then have 'OVERNIGHT BAG' in the centre, with individual items (toothpaste, etc.) radiating from it. Indeed, this sub-ordinate bubble might be standard for all the one-day conferences this speaker addresses.

Logical connections

Once all the ideas are recorded and linked together, their order can be considered. In this simple example, there are three obvious stages which fall into a logical time sequence:

1. Advance preparation

2. Packing

3. On arrival

These 'key' bubbles (indicated by broken circles) have become apparent as the ideas are linked (the ideas being in completed circles). Different colours for different stages of organization are often helpful. Some bubbles clearly generate sub-divisions: 2. Packing contains personal items such as the overnight bag and 'briefcase' property needed at the conference itself, such as overhead transparencies. These items form subordinate bubbles, the equivalent of sub-sections. Each section and sub-section could, in a report, be given a suitable heading and appropriate decimal number (see Chapter 3). The contents list can then be put together and eventually the sections will be written. The writing itself need not begin at the beginning, as each section can be identified and written as a separate entity (although some final checking for consistency will be needed: see Chapter 6). A light crossing-out will mark each completed section or bubble, and illustrations can be noted as belonging to each section of writing.

Spider 'notes'

Illustrations are not the only additional items which can be noted alongside the spider diagram. A useful 'tool' is a clear space of paper on which can be recorded information which must be included in detail and which cannot be summarized in a key word or phrase. Such information might include people's names, amounts of money, formulae or references. It is often helpful to use A3 paper folded in half, with the spider on one half and the detailed notes opposite. However the spider diagram is organized, it will almost certainly look messy and be personal to its owner (it could probably be tidied up for someone else to look at, but this is secondary to its main purpose of helping its creator to organize ideas). Your colleagues may make unwelcome comments about those who draw lots of 'doodles' on pieces of paper before 'getting down to the job'; ignore them. You are involved in the serious work of preparing the ideas from which your report will eventually be structured and written.

Nevertheless, when the office is full of piles of information and the desk top is crawling with spiders, you may be tempted to start writing. This would be like starting to build before looking at the architect's plans: not impossible, but hazardous. Reports need to be designed, and the structure must be planned in detail before the words can be put in position. Essentially, reports need beginnings and endings, and a logical sequence in between, and the rest of this chapter and Chapter 3 will show how the different departments of a report are joined to make a whole building. In general terms, the stages described are in the order in which the report writer will work at them, from the linking of ideas in the spider diagram to the detailed organization of the summary, title page and references, but the order may vary with the needs of a particular report. Planning, however, is always the first step.

Beginning and ending

Beginning at the beginning can have its uses, but the problem as it faces the report writer is to identify the beginning. Boring the reader with a great deal of information which is already known is as bad as beginning in the middle and so leaving the reader in total confusion about why the report was needed at all. The latter mistake is usually that of the expert who has worked on the subject of the report for many years and who knows the background and the particular problem so well that it seems impossible that there exists a reader who does not share this knowledge. So, reasonably from this point of view, understanding is assumed and the writer gets straight to the solution of the problem, leaving the reader wondering why it was a problem in the first place.

Making assumptions about the reader or readers of a report is a dangerous activity. The writer of a good report will have checked, before beginning to gather information, the reader's technical expertise, knowledge of the subject of the report, and experience of the problem under discussion (knowledge being, of course, very different from experience). With this information in mind, the writer can start to plan the beginning of the report, what needs to be explained and what can sensibly be taken for granted, so that the reader is neither patronized nor bewildered. If the writer is sure that much background information is shared, then indeed the report can start somewhere in the middle, but it must be clear that not only is the knowledge shared with the intended reader, but also that other readers who might be interested are not puzzled by the absence of explanation. Reports may lie in a drawer for a long time, to be taken out by the original reader's successor, who must also understand what is written. Knowing who the reader is, who the other likely readers are, and what they all know about the subject, will determine where the report begins.

In the same way, a decision must be made about the end of a report. It is rarely the end of the story: there will be discussions, meetings, perhaps further reports, and action taken as a result of the report when it is presented. Indeed, the experiments themselves may continue, and the project lead on to a further project, so that the point at which the original report finished is no longer clear. The writer must decide how much the reader needs to know, whether the report is a progress report or a final report, what time constraints must be borne in mind, and in the light of these decisions the report can be concluded, as long as the reader is aware if there is more to follow.

Between the beginning and the end come the logical stages. These are necessary, as we showed in Chapter 1, to meet the needs of the report user, the person who will pick and choose which sections to read, which to skim, and which to ignore. The general pattern is clear to the writer once the spiders are drawn and the sections of information identified: the detailed format must now be organized for the sake of that all-important person, the reader.

Key points in Chapter 2

- Choose an appropriate procedure and collect all relevant facts.

- Give the facts objectively, draw your Conclusions and make your own Recommendations.

- Design and plan the report before starting to write it (a spider diagram is recommended).

- Assumptions are dangerous—*check* where to begin and where to end.

CHAPTER 3

Format

*Contents lists · Headings · Numbering systems · Pagination · Appendices ·
Review of headings · Conclusions and Recommendations · References and
bibliography · Summaries · Title page · Binding*

Contents lists

As we discussed at the end of the previous chapter, the organization of a report, its format, must be clearly defined long before
the writing begins. From the earliest stages of the work, the writer
must think in terms of sections and headings, and one of the first
sections to be written will be the contents list. This may seem surprising, but a provisional list of headings produces a guide to the
more detailed organization, and it is flexible: the writer can move
headings round on a page more easily than reorganize whole sections of writing.

Some companies, particularly those with quality systems such as
BS5750 accredited procedures, prescribe a format for all their reports.
Indeed, some actually provide a format within their information technology systems, so that the writer is prompted by the computer to put
all the data into the required pattern. However, even these systems
usually leave the choice of headings, or at least of sub-headings, to the
author, and rightly so, as the words used must describe the specific
material included as accurately as possible. We have assumed such
freedom in this chapter.

First of all, the writer must return to the spider mentioned previously. This animal, as described, is a useful aid to the accumulation
of ideas and the formation of links between them. It is also helpful in
providing the headings which will appear in the contents list, for a

word or phrase often becomes clear as the general summary of an 'area' of spider. At first, these summary words will usually be vague and wide in scope: 'Background', 'Site Visit', 'Results' are adequate to begin with, although they are too imprecise for the final report. A contents list can still be drawn up at this stage, even if it looks in part like this:

Background

    Terms of reference

    Own previous work ========= Experimental
                        ========= Already published

    Others' published work

    Aim of this investigation

Nobody could pretend that this is an adequate contents list for a report, but it shows the beginning of a plan of action, and a logical pattern for the report to take. If the writer then decides that other people's published work should be considered first, the order of the headings can easily be changed—only a moment's work. Changing whole chunks of a written report takes much longer. The precision at which the headings must eventually arrive is discussed later in this chapter, and shown in the worked short reports (see pages 91 and 102). Sometimes, the main sections are known to the writer, who can start to pattern headings and sub-headings easily. For example, the writer of a report on insulation will be aware that when house insulation is considered, three main areas will emerge: the walls, the windows and the loft. If House Insulation is the third section of the report, the first contents list might be something like:

3. House Insulation
   Walls
         Cavity
         Dry lining
         Pebble dashing

   Windows
         Double glazing

Loft
    Types
    Materials used

The section on loft insulation is vague, and more detailed thought will have to be given to the headings later, but the organization is becoming clear. As long as the contents list is subsequently revised and checked, it is a highly important piece of work achieved, and the report writer can feel a sense of satisfaction with just one page which sets out how the report will be organized and the logic of that organization. However, for most report writers, detailed headings are still in the future, and a standard format appropriate to the report is the first stage in the making of the contents.

Headings

The number and type of headings used will be determined by the length, complexity and formality of the report: sometimes Introduction, Findings, Comments will be sufficient. Company rules may make other headings obligatory, or the report material in itself may need specific treatment. For instance, *a pure science laboratory report* might use the following:

Abstract
Introduction (literature and current state of research)
Materials and methods (experimental design)
Results (including both statistics and, if appropriate, comments)
Discussion (of the writer's own data, put in the context of other published work)
Conclusions
Summary
References.

A report which examines and considers *a technical process* might have headings such as:

Introduction (including the background to and reason for the investigation)
Summary (including the main recommendations)
Procedure (how the tests were carried out)
Results (facts only)

Discussion (the implications of the testing)
Conclusions (what is acceptable/not acceptable, and why)
Recommendations (based on the conclusions).

If the *report is advisory*, with lengthy factual and discursive material, it may need the full 'standard' format, which would contain the following sections:

Title page
Acknowledgements
Summary
Analytical contents list (sections and page numbers)
Terms of reference/Introduction (why the report was written, and for whom)
Procedure (how the information was obtained)
Findings (the facts which were obtained)
Conclusions (the implications of what has been revealed)
Recommendations (what should happen as a result of the report)
References (books, journals, etc., mentioned in the report)
Bibliography (other useful background reading)
Appendices (supplementary material).

All these headings may be omitted or adapted in any individual report, but they are a useful aid to the writer in suggesting a pattern for the report and a guide to the organization. Most everyday reports will not need such detailed treatment, but a formal, published report might indeed have all the above sections.

The report writer now has a framework for the report, and some ideas for headings, probably within the <u>Procedure</u> and <u>Findings</u> sections. Whether the actual headings <u>Procedure</u> and <u>Findings</u>, or indeed any other of the headings listed above, are used or not depends on the report. They are more likely to turn into precise words which will help the reader to find the way through the report material. Most report users start by selecting what is most important or urgent, on the basis of the information in the contents list. The writer must help the reader to identify such material rapidly and accurately, by providing precise headings.

Once the headings are ordered, even provisionally, the material will fit more easily into place, and the more detailed the preliminary organization is, the easier the writing will be. This stage of report preparation is often rushed, the writer being understandably anxious to get down to the 'real' job of writing the report, but problems can be foreseen and so avoided if time is given to the organization. A 'jump' in the logical pattern of headings suggests that a sub-section may have been omitted and more information should be given at that point while a large number of sub-headings might suggest that too much information is being forced under one main heading. Flexibility of headings and of material is essential until the writer is happy with the contents list (still provisional) and the way in which it reveals how the material is logically organized.

Numbering systems

As the logic of the report is seen in the headings, so it is also apparent in the notation. All reports have a numbering system of some kind, whether simple:

1. Introduction
2. Findings
3. Comments

or the more complex but highly recommended decimal notation system. Numbers and headings are linked: each number will have a heading beside it to show where it fits into the report pattern. It is helpful to have a system which is widely used and easily recognized, which is one of the two great advantages of decimal notation, the other being the logic which is inherent in it. If a mixed system is used, the reader will find it difficult to decide whether (b) comes before or after (iii) and how it relates to (A). It will also be hard to identify a single section with its sub-sections, and this will be a greater problem for the report user than for the report reader. Roman numerals (i, ii, iii, etc.) should always be avoided, as many people find them difficult to work out, and they are liable to be confused with letters.

Decimal notation

Decimal notation avoids all these problems. The major sections are given single arabic numbers (1, 2, 3, etc.) in sequential order; the first level of sub-section will follow a decimal point (1.1), and the first sub-section under that sub-section will repeat the process (1.1.1). It is possible to sub-divide many times, but for practical purposes four numbers is the maximum, and three will often be sufficient. The use of a string of numbers (1.1.3.4.6, etc.) suggests that the material has not been well organized; in the course of handling very many technical reports, we have not found an example of a well-constructed report which has used more than three levels of numbers after the decimal point.

The reader will be further helped if the form of the headings agrees with the decimal hierarchy, and reinforces it. If the major number has the boldest heading (upper case, bold type), then the first level sub-division will have a form of heading which is clearly subordinate (initial capitals, bold, small type size), and this reinforcement of the hierarchy can continue for as long as there are forms available to differentiate between the levels. If we look back to the report on systems of insulation, again assuming that House Insulation is the third section, we can see how the three areas mentioned, walls, loft and windows, will be organized.

3. HOUSE INSULATION

....

3.1 Walls

3.1.1 Cavity filling

....

....

3.1.2 Dry lining

....

....

3.1.3 Pebble dashing

....

....

3.2 Loft

....

....

3.2.1 Fibre glass

....

3.2.2 Polystyrene tiles

....

....

3.3 Windows
3.3.1 Double glazing

....
....

3.3.2 Brick over

....

Some headings will have information immediately under them (as **3.2 Loft** has) and some will move from major heading to subordinate heading (as 3.1 is followed at once by 3.1.1): the material available is the criterion. The advantage of this system is that if the report user is interested only in loft insulation, it is obvious from the contents list where this section is located, that it begins at 3.2 and that it ends at 3.3. The contents list will give at least the first two levels of heading, together with the page numbers.

In the text, each heading should be on a new line, and the section or sub-section under it should also start on a new line, so that the heading can be easily located. In a long report, major sections may start on a new page, possibly with their own sectional contents list under the major heading.

Numbering lists

Occasionally, the writer may require a list of items to be included in the decimal notation system, without wanting the individual items in the list to be identified separately. A report which discussed life cycle costing in construction[3] introduced the basis for costing an individual building with a series of questions:

- Where it is located?
- Are there any drawings available?
- What is the breakdown of the functional floor areas?
- What is the general construction?
- What is its general condition?
- When was it built?

There are many more questions, all dealt with later in the report, but the introductory list is not in itself referred to. The items are therefore 'bulleted', identified by a large black dot to the left of each item, easily seen but not requiring a level of decimal notation. If it is necessary to list items and to refer to them individually, they can be identified by arabic numbers in brackets to the left of the item. The questions listed above could have been handled in this way if it had been found necessary to comment on them, for instance:

(1)   Where is it located?
(2)   Are there any drawings available?
(3)   What is the breakdown of the functional floor areas?

and, at the end of the list, perhaps:

Question (1) is important, as local climatic conditions affect the materials used . . .

Again, the items can be identified without the need for further decimal numbering.

Paragraph numbering

In this chapter, we have stressed the value of decimal notation, as both logical and widely used. However, other forms of notation are sometimes found, one of them especially in Government reports. This is the numbering of every paragraph throughout the report. It can be useful if the whole work is short, and likely to be the subject of meetings and telephone discussions, when the need to identify a small quantity of material quickly is imperative. It is, on the other hand, not logical, except that paragraph 647 is found between 646 and 648. The reader cannot tell whether paragraph 647 is more general and introductory than 648, or whether a new major section of the report begins at 649. It is impossible to extract a major section and know at once that it is complete, as the reader could know that section 6.4 began at 6.4 and ended at 6.5.

A side-effect of using paragraph numbering is the production of very long paragraphs, the writer being unwilling to create an artificial sub-division by starting a new paragraph and so continuing the current one for three-quarters of a page! Decimal notation, of course, allows for several paragraphs under the same heading, if it is appropriate. With the minor exception of the very short report discussed orally, there seems little to recommend the paragraph style of numbering. It does not even produce a satisfactory contents list, as headings can be listed but their relative importance cannot be seen in the notation.

Pagination

Reference has already been made to page numbers. Surprisingly, many reports appear without page numbers, sometimes as a result of poor photocopying (the number was on the original, but disappeared from the top or bottom of the page in the copying) but often because nobody thought to add the numbers. Pagination is, of course, a facility on wordprocessors, but it may be overlooked, especially if the system requires it to be set up *before* the document is written. Otherwise, the page numbering can be added at the end, in one sequence throughout the report.

'Throughout' is an important word in the previous sentence, as some reports have different sequences in their paging: roman numerals are often used for the preliminary pages, and a new sequence is sometimes introduced for each appendix. Pages which are entirely diagrammatic in content are occasionally omitted entirely from the numbering, with dire results. All pages which follow the title page, contents list and summary should be included in one sequence, and the page numbers will appear, of course, on the final contents list.

Appendices

So far, we have considered material which is in category A only (see Chapter 2), but the pile of information in the B category (more or less relevant, or relevant to some readers if not all) has also been growing. This was considered as material for the appendix and, if the report writer has not decided otherwise, that is where it will appear. Appendices are the writer's friends, allowing the inclusion of information which is not in the mainstream of the report but which cannot be ignored. They are also a partial answer to the most difficult of problems, the diverse readership. They represent the last resting place of that which is borderline-relevant or of interest to the specialist only.

The terms of reference of a report may ask the writer to consider three possible ways of heating a building. In the findings, the writer has investigated each method, looked at its installation and maintenance costs, its efficiency, and its general suitability for the building involved. The conclusions have shown the difference between the three types, pointing out that while Type X is expensive and difficult to install, its running costs will be lower than those of Type Y, which is much easier to install. The human race being what it is, the people who work in the building are all clamouring for Type Z, which is expensive to install and to run, but which is efficient, quiet and flexible to seasonal changes of temperature. The report writer has looked at all the pros and cons and, with a sigh of relief at being only the report writer and not having to live with the consequences, has recommended Type X. The staff will get used to it (having little option) and it will be economical to run.

So the recommendation is Type X, for all the appropriate reasons, and the report writer is left with a mass of detailed material about the running costs of Types Y and Z. Clearly, these are not irrelevant to the report, but equally obviously, more detail will be given about Type X, with enough information to show why it will eventually be cheaper than the other two. This is a clear case for the use of appendices. The detailed examples of the method and the cost of using Types Y and Z will become Appendix A and Appendix B (it is useful to give appendices letters rather than numbers, to keep them separate from the main part of the report). When, after many meetings and much lengthy discussion, the general manager decides on Type Z (after all, a manager has to work with the company employees every day and to put up with their complaints), the information needed will be available at the end of the report. If, two years later, anyone complains about the cost of the new heating system, all the evidence is available to show what a dreadful mistake was made, and while this may be unfortunate for the general manager, the report writer is exonerated.

The general manager may decide to move on, and some years later a successor will be faced with the rising costs of heating the building and will wonder why on earth such a crazy decision was made in the first place. The report will provide the evidence, if not the answer to the problem, and this is another aspect of the usefulness of appendices. They provide the back-up information which is invaluable to those who follow the original decision-makers, and ensure that, with luck, the same mistakes are not made again.

Appendices are also of use to the specialist reader. Our old friend the insulation report is a useful example. The main material of the report deals with the insulation of public buildings, libraries and town halls, and, in Section 3, with the insulation of houses. The report user reads Section 3, and is dubious. It all makes sense in theory, but what about the limited budget? Some worked examples are needed which include an ordinary three-bedroomed house and which show the percentage gained if only one area can be insulated. There in the appendices are the examples, and it is clear that double glazing, although useful, will not save as much in heating costs as will loft insulation. In the same way, experimental data which are of interest only to the expert reader can usefully be presented in an appendix, as can supporting statistics, or maps and charts (but for a more detailed discussion of the position of diagrammatic material, see Chapter 5). The main text remains uncluttered with detail not needed by most readers, while that detail is available for the few readers who will need it.

If it is necessary to sub-divide an appendix, the sections can follow a decimal notation pattern preceded by the appendix letter. So B3.1 is the first sub-division of the third section of Appendix B. Needless to say, so much detailed division is rarely necessary. The appendices are, nevertheless, an integral part of the report, listed in the contents and included in the page numbering.

Review of headings

Once the main text plan is established and the order of appendices decided, much of the preparatory work is done. By this time, some small factual sections of the report are written, and the whole structure is becoming clear and logically expressed. Headings must be checked for accuracy and for precision, and again the contents list is useful. The report writer should go back to the contents and ask what the reader would expect to find under each of the headings. 'Services' might have been a useful starting place, but what does it suggest? Bus, train, church, tennis, after-sales, gas and electricity, or the army, navy and air force? The word is much too wide in its implications to be used as a heading without further definition. The length and complexity of sections should also be again revised: are more—or fewer—sub-divisions needed? The organization of the report must be revised regularly until the clearest, most precise and helpful headings are found, and the logic of the whole made obvious and accessible to the reader.

Titles

A further word is needed on the subject of headings and, indeed, report titles. Precision is crucially important, for the sake of the report writer as well as the reader, for a vague title probably means that the report will be overlooked, and it is disheartening to spend time and effort only to find one's work neglected. As a rule, it is better to have a short title than a long one: it is more easily remembered, it attracts the attention more readily, and it is easier to identify, especially if a company's reports are filed by keywords on the computer. Sometimes, however, a title will have to be lengthy simply because to shorten it would be to change its meaning or its scope. A useful compromise can be a very short title followed by a longer, more explanatory sub-title, as in the Cockcroft Report (HMSO, 1982):

Mathematics Counts

Report of the Committee of Inquiry into the teaching of
mathematics in schools

The short title succeeds in attracting attention, while the longer sub-title gives precise information about the subject of the report. As with most writing, the author must sit back and look at the title and the headings as dispassionately as possible. Questions as headings tend to downgrade a report to the level of leaflets which fall on the doormat, asking 'Why not double glaze your windows?' to which there is either no reply because talking to a leaflet seems ridiculous or a useless reply such as 'Because I've done so already!' This is not as far-fetched an analogy as it sounds, since asking questions in a report heading has just the same effect: there is no way readers can answer, and in any case they are reading the report precisely because they are interested in the subject and will ask the questions themselves. There is also the problem of unintentional humour:

The growth of timber framed houses

is a good title in principle, but suggests inevitably that little timber framed houses grow into bigger timber framed houses, which might be useful for their owners. An analysis of the different sections of a particular company's internal communications network ended up with the following heading:

The breakdown of the telephone system

thus giving rise to suggestions of trouble where there was none. Clearly, titles need serious consideration by report writers, as does the choice of an appropriate file reference so that the report which is stored in the company's system can be easily identified.

Conclusions and Recommendations

The organization of the main findings of the report will follow the pattern suggested above, with its appropriate headings and notation. The conclusions are there to bring together material which, although scattered through the findings, can be identified as presenting a common aspect which sums up much that has gone before: on the basis of the evidence, the writer concludes that certain problems have been identified. In the recommendations, if they are asked for, ways of solving the problems will be suggested, and one or more particularly important or urgent solutions stressed. Both conclusions and recommendations continue the headings and notation pattern of the earlier part of the report, and the writer must be sure that no new evidence which was not revealed in the findings appears at this late stage. The evidence must, in the main body of the text, precede the conclusions.

Recommendations are not always asked for in the terms of reference, and many reports end with the conclusions. Sometimes in-company or inter-company politics mean that recommendations have to be hinted at rather than stated clearly, and as usual the policy of the writer's organization is binding on the writer. However, where both conclusions and recommendations appear, they must be kept separate. In principle, the conclusions are an objective assessment of the facts, while the recommendations are the writer's subjective view of how the facts should be dealt with, but in practice the subjective/objective distinction is blurred. In selecting some facts and rejecting others, in considering the evidence, the writer is inevitably subjective. Nevertheless, the recommendations are the ideas of the writer, who bears responsibility for their implications, which is, indeed, one of the principal reasons for the signing and dating of all reports. The writer accepts responsibility, and often a superior in the organization will in turn accept responsibility by also signing as ratification of what has been produced and sometimes also to signify permission for the document to be released.

A simple example will illustrate the distinction between the conclusions and the recommendations. In an old office building, there is a rather steep staircase with an awkward turn in it. One winter afternoon, an employee, carrying a large pile of papers, falls on the stairs and breaks an arm. An accident report form is completed, but the office manager feels that further investigation is needed, and asks a member of the personnel staff to have a closer look at the circumstances in which the incident took place. It becomes clear that there have been a number of minor complaints about the difficulty of negotiating the staircase, especially in poor light, comments that the stair carpet is becoming worn in places (although not yet dangerous in itself), and a general feeling that the employee was negligent in knowing of the hazard and yet trying to carry so large an amount of paper that the view of the staircase was impaired. The conclusions of the report were therefore that:

1. the staircase was awkward when natural light was not good;

2. the state of the carpet did not contribute to the accident, but it was worn in places;

3. the accident was caused in part by the amount of paper being carried at the time;

4. previous complaints about the staircase had not resulted in action.

These are conclusions based on investigation and, probably, interview. They are objective facts, and do not in themselves suggest action to be taken: they follow from the evidence presented.

When the writer turns to the recommendations, an assessment has to be made of action to be taken as a result of these conclusions. The light on the staircase is obviously a problem, and extra light fittings with stronger bulbs or fluorescent strips might be recommended. A potential hazard in the form of the carpet has been revealed, and the writer might well suggest *at this point in the report* that the carpet should be replaced and that in choosing the colour, the problem of visibility should be taken into account. Such a suggestion is the writer's own, based on the conclusions but in no way hinted at within the conclusions section. How much is recommended about the third and fourth conclusions will depend on an overall view of the situation: do staff normally carry quantities of paper down the stairs, and if so, should they be warned to be careful, and is there a wider implication that reasonable complaints by the staff are ignored by those responsible for health and safety at work? Further recommendations may be called for, or, on the other hand, it may be assumed that the incident is unlikely to be repeated and that reasonable channels for complaint had been ignored by the staff, in spite of general awareness that the channels existed. Obviously, this is a simplistic example, as such an incident would in reality involve, for example, the union safety representative, but the pattern is clear: conclusions are a consideration of the evidence while recommendations suggest action as a result of such consideration, and they are normally kept apart.

References and bibliography

By the time that the report writer has completed the introduction, findings, conclusions and recommendations, and organized the appendices of the report, most of the work is done. There remain a few aspects of the format of the report which still need consideration, and one of these will have been kept in mind since the report was begun. Many reports have neither references nor a bibliography, but some have either or both, and the preparation of these sections will continue through the organization and writing of the rest of the report. References show the published (or occasionally non-published) work which has been used in the writing, quoted from and specifically mentioned, and there are accepted ways of showing both the textual mark and the full details of the sources. A bibliography is a list of published work (again, occasionally non-published, for instance a thesis) which has not been specifically referred to in the text, but which will be of interest and use to the reader. If both are included in a report, they must be in separate lists, the references first, usually in the order in which they occur in the text, and then the bibliography, usually in alphabetical order of author or body responsible for the production of the item.

A reference, once forgotten, is difficult to recall. As soon as it is apparent that books, journals, other reports and similar material will be used or mentioned in the text, the writer should start to prepare the lists which will form the bases of the bibliographical sections. All the details recorded must be correct, and it is always wise to record all useful material: it is much easier to reject an item later than to hunt for missing information. Report writers are normally responsible for checking the copyright position of material quoted, and if necessary obtaining written permission to quote. As a reference is recorded, the text should be marked to remind the writer to complete the textual mark as appropriate.

Most references come from one or more of the five kinds of source:

books
journals
published reports
conference proceedings
reports produced by the writer's own company

Various kinds of textual mark are possible; one which is commonly used is the superscript arabic number, as in the following example:

A study published recently[4] shows that current research ...

However, in the case of reports with a high percentage of mathematical material—and perhaps more generally in recent years—the Harvard System is preferred. This requires the author's name, date of publication and page reference to appear in brackets in the text, as follows:

A study published recently (Bloggs 2001, p. 256) shows ...

Either of these styles is acceptable, but company policy may dictate a particular form, as may the nature of the report material. Consistency is essential, whichever form is chosen.

Consistency is also necessary in the full form of the reference at the end of the report. Common forms of references are given below, but if a different form is chosen, the writer must be careful to include all important information, and to be consistent in the layout. Usually the references will be in the order in which they occur in the report, and the numbers will therefore be sequential. The examples given are, clearly, fictitious!

Example 1 Book Reference
14 Bloggs, J., *Electronics for All*, McGraw-Hill, 15th edn, 2003.

or, if the Harvard System is used,

14 Bloggs, J., 2003, *Electronics for All*, McGraw-Hill, 15th edn.

Example 2 Journal Reference
19 Bloggs, J., 'Electronics for the undergraduate', *Electronic World*, **88**, August 2001, p. 16–29.

Example 3 Report Reference
96 Bloggs, Judith, *Working in electronics*, April 2010, National Engineering Laboratory, NEL, Report no. 999.

Example 4 Conference Proceedings Reference
102 Bloggs, James,, 'Communication courses for engineers', in *The Education of an Engineer*, Conference Proceedings, University of Reading, 1 April 2009, pp. 222–233.

In the case of reference to reports produced by the writer's own company, the organization's standard policy should be followed; if the report is published, the publishers will give guidance about the correct form of reference. As a general rule, words in italics will be those which appear on the spine of a published book.

It is always sensible to give as much information as possible, including the most complete form of the author's name. Various members of a family may publish books on related subjects (as indicated by the fictitious Bloggs family), and the particular author should be identified. If there are two authors, both names will be given:

21 Bloggs, Judith and Amanda Bloggs, *The Growth of the Electronics Industry: a Historic Survey*, McGraw-Hill, 2nd edn, 2015.

However, if there are more than two authors, it is customary to give the first only, indicating that others exist:

46 Bloggs, J., *et al.*, *Electronics in the Twenty-first Century*, McGraw-Hill, 2004.

The date is essential in all references: books go out of date quickly, especially in the field of technology, and the reader will judge the value of the report partly by the dates of the references (and by the edition number, particularly when a book has rapidly run to several editions). References must always be checked, as few things are more frustrating to a reader than to hunt for a reference and be unable to find it, perhaps for as simple a reason as transposed page numbers. Above all, the writer should give accurate information, and be consistent in the chosen format.

Much of what has been said about references applies also to the bibliography. The information should be as full as possible and consistent, but the items are usually listed in alphabetical order of author, the details being given in the forms suggested in the examples above. There are, of course, no textual marks as the works listed have not been specifically mentioned in the text.

Summaries

There remains in the preparation of a report the report writer's nightmare, the summary. This has to be the final section written, and in some ways it is the most difficult. In a small space (perhaps 10 or 12 lines of print for a report of 50 or 60 pages), the author has to give a miniaturized picture of the report not only for the report reader, but also for those who will never set eyes on the whole report.

Uses of the summary

The summary has grown in importance in recent years. Originally, it was intended as an overall view of the report, and it still serves this purpose. It is also a reminder of the essentials of the report for the readers who have read the whole work but who need to have their memories refreshed, perhaps before going to a meeting at which the subject of the report is discussed. It also shows the report user how each section fits into the report as a whole. However, the summary has another, and more delicate, task. It will probably take on a life of its own, independent of the rest of the report, and be circulated to a number of people who have a general interest in the subject but who have neither time nor inclination to read the report. (These include people who feel that their status demands that they have a general interest in the subject, even if they haven't, or who feel that they need to have an overall view of what is going on in the company.) For this reason, the summary is not usually included in the pagination of the report, although it will appear in the contents: a copy of the summary or summaries must be bound into the report, even if its real service is as a separate entity.

Summary contents

The summary page usually includes the report title, with or without reference number, and the date, with any other code which will identify the whole report or show its confidentiality. Otherwise, the summary should stand alone. It will give the reader a clear and balanced view of what the report is about, and will stress the most important or most urgent aspects of the conclusions and/or recommendations. While it gives a balanced view of the report, it is not a balanced representation of the whole, and in this it differs from a précis, which reproduces all the major thoughts of the original passage with the same stress that they had in the original. The report summary has to explain enough of the background to be intelligible to the reader who will not see the whole thing, but its greatest value is in bringing to the readers' attention that which they most need to know, that is, what has been concluded or recommended in the light of the evidence in the report.

The report writer, then, might usefully begin preparation of the summary by sitting back and considering what are the most important aspects of the report, that is, what aspects, if the report were to combust spontaneously, should most urgently be saved. These essentials should then be drafted in a few sentences, emphasizing what action must be taken immediately. At this stage, it might be helpful to list the points to be included, numbering them as far as possible in order of priority. The reader's point of view has then to be considered. How can the context of these few important sentences be made clear to the reader who has no access to the full report? This information must also be written briefly, although it is better to include too much material than not enough. As with précis writing, it is much easier to cut a passage which is too long than to extend a passage which is too short. These two sections, the background and the essential recommendations, have next to be knitted together to read as a whole piece of prose, with 'link words' (see Chapter 4) to guide the reader. There is, however, no need to keep the final summary in one paragraph (again, unlike a précis); if two or three short paragraphs are more helpful than one long one, then divide up the writing.

If the preparation of the summary has been well done, the result will be unambiguous and accurate, but too long. Now the writer can look for the wordy expression ('in the first instance' is the same as but longer than 'firstly'), cut out repetition, and omit any detail which, on reflection, seems inessential. This is probably a good time at which to ask a colleague to read the summary to see if it makes sense or if some necessary information has been left out. It is clear by now that the writing of the summary cannot be left for the last ten minutes: it is a complicated piece of work, and, as it is the first section of the report to be read, it must be impressive.

Earlier in this chapter an example was given of conclusions and recommendations, in a report on the circumstances and site of an accident on an office staircase. We can use the same information as an example of how the report summary would be written. The writer would mention the accident (but without details), and the place where it happened. Since the report is not concerned with the accident itself, the time and the poor natural light would not be important, and although the apparent neglect of complaints made is in itself important, the recommendations would show whether it had proved worthy of further investigation. Most of the summary would therefore deal with the need to improve the lighting and to replace worn carpeting before it became a hazard. If the writer had concluded that more safety notices were needed, or that there should be better communication of potential dangers between staff and management, then these points would also appear in the summary. The need for urgent action might also be stressed. So the summary would clarify the need for the investigation, but principally would show (perhaps for the benefit of other departments in other parts of the building) what recommendations had been made.

Title page

There remains the title page, which may not be the writer's responsibility, if the company uses a standard format. However, the author should beware the overcrowded title page. A good layout is important, for the first impression the report makes is by its appearance, on the shelf or desk (when the binding will, or will fail to, impress) and when it is opened and the reader looks at the first page. Some information is essential: the title, the name of the author or group responsible for the production of the report, and the date. Other information will appear because of the organization to which the writer belongs: the company name, perhaps the logo and address, a reference number by which the report is identified, and sometimes also the signature of the senior manager responsible for the approval and distribution of the report. Apart from any classification such as 'Confidential', there should be nothing more on the title page, as a crowded page looks untidy and tends to distract from what the reader is most likely to read, the author and title of the report. Distribution lists are better kept on a separate sheet or, if necessary, added on the verso of the title page. Placing the summary on the title page, which is occasionally done in order to save paper, is not recommended.

Dates

Two of the items mentioned in the previous paragraph need emphasis. The date must appear on the report, and most suitably on the title page. The presence of the date is to some extent a safety net for the writer, who is responsible for the contents of the report on that date. If subsequent legal or financial or other changes invalidate the recommendations, then (assuming that such an eventuality could not have been foreseen) the author cannot be held responsible for what happened after that date. An undated report can be a time-bomb for its author. The date is also necessary for future readers. The authors of this book have seen test reports on machinery which could kill or seriously injure its operator, and the reports have been undated. It is surely essential for the operators to know whether the tests are recent, or 10 years out of date and possibly invalidated by more recent research. A report without a date should never be allowed to pass from writer to reader, whether inside or outside the writer's company.

Confidential reports

Problems are also sometimes caused by the classification of documents. Terms such as 'Confidential' should be used only when they are strictly necessary, or they are degraded in impact. If they are used, they should be used in such a way that the classification is immediately obvious, that is, on the cover if possible, and certainly on the title page and on all pages of text. It is too easy to use the word once, often in the top left-hand corner of the title page where it can be overlooked, and forget that in the nature of reports, the user may not look at the beginning first. In the case of restricted reports, the copy number may be needed (Copy 3 of 6, for example), and if an organization has its own code to show the restriction of a report, that code should always be adhered to, and should always be apparent on the report itself.

Binding

The binding of a report is perhaps not strictly part of the format, but most companies have a policy, more or less followed, about the bindings to be used for different sorts of report. Expensive and impressive reports will sometimes go to a designer (wisely, as a typographer, for instance, will make the best impact with the report material), and will be professionally bound. Spiral bindings are often favoured for smaller reports, and they have the advantage of allowing the pages to open flat, which is particularly useful if there are many diagrams. Slide bar binding is common for internal reports: it is cheap and looks satisfactory, but it often makes opening the report difficult and can be irritating in use. Ring binders are bulky, but in many ways more satisfactory. Companies often have a company colour which is used for all external reports, and sometimes a different colour for internal reports. Whatever cover is chosen, it should be easy for the reader to use, should hold the pages firmly in place so that none gets lost, and should look attractive.

Text, binding and cover combine to interest the reader and to hold the attention. They should therefore be considered together, as the results of producing the text without reference to the binding can be disastrous, with holes punched through essential numbers, and the beginnings of words disappearing into the binding. The commonly-used plastic cover with a 'window' through which the title of the report and its author's name appear is sensible and reasonable in price, but this information must be accurately positioned. Years of work spent writing reports without the gratification of seeing one's name in print does nothing for the writer's confidence.

In all that has been written in this chapter about the format of reports, it is obvious that the reader's convenience is the paramount consideration, as it is also in the writing and in the diagrammatic presentation. Flexibility is therefore necessary, and company policy, usually the overriding force, should allow for some variation in style, layout and organization if the result will be an increase of goodwill. Failure to consider the total impact can result in lack of credibility, as the following real-life comment on a tender document shows:

The fact that (the company's) later submissions were presented in a very muddled form does not inspire confidence in this contractor.

Key points in Chapter 3

- Start with the Contents list, and plan the order of headings and sub-headings.

- Use precise headings to guide the reader through the information and to allow accurate and rapid selection of material.

- Check that the numbering system reinforces the logical order of headings (decimal notation is recommended).

- Ensure that all pages are numbered, preferably in one sequence through the report.

- Use appendices to clear the main text of supporting or specialist material which most readers won't want to see.

- Remember that short titles are memorable.

- Draw Conclusions which show the implications of the evidence, and make Recommendations which show what should be done about it.

- All your references should be informative, accurate and consistent in style.

- Make sure that the Summary highlights—briefly—the most important/urgent aspects of the report; it may be all that some readers will ever look at.

- Always date your reports; use 'Confidential' only if you really mean it.

- Your final check will be to make sure that text, binding and cover combine to interest the reader and to hold the attention.

CHAPTER 4

Words, words

Words · Sentences · Punctuation · Grammar · Worked example of confused expression · Paragraphs · Style · List of commonly mis-used words

Words

'Words, words, words,' commented Hamlet, thus expressing the despair of many report writers and incidentally also their habit of saying the same thing three times. Words undoubtedly cause difficulties, not least by taking on a life of their own and being understood in different ways by different readers.

Hamlet and his creator had a way with words, using them not only fluently but also beautifully. Reports are not, generally speaking, read for their literary qualities, but they must be unambiguous, grammatically correct and as easy as possible to read. In this last respect, Shakespeare and the average report writer have one thing in common: the craft of writing. Contrary to popular belief, good writing is not merely a gift of nature, although it is undoubtedly easier for some people than for others. It is also a craft, and a good writer, whether of plays or reports, will work at writing, revising, changing, worrying at a sentence or a paragraph until it is as well written as possible, which means as readable as possible.

The usual objection to this is that time gets in the way of good writing, and even of accurate writing. If the report is needed by senior management before the end of the afternoon, the writer cannot spend time polishing up its style, however desirable that might be. This is, of course, a valid objection, but a writer who is aware of the requirements of good style and the pitfalls of bad, will think about the art of writing when there *is* time and will also notice something which is well written. The technical skills will be practised whenever possible, noticed whenever the opportunity arises, and will gradually become a habit. It will then become apparent that a well written report creates goodwill in the reader, does not create lawsuits because it was ambiguous, and generally brings credit to the writer's company. Good writing, in fact, has become good management and cost-effective, too.

However, Hamlet's habit of repetition resulted from dramatic and psychological necessity: the report writer's from lack of confidence. Writers who are not sure of the reader's comprehension, often consider repeating the idea in different words. Indeed some writers become carried away by this technique, repeating the same idea again and again, and wasting everybody's time. If the idea is expressed precisely and concisely at the first writing, both writer and reader are happy.

This chapter, then, will look first at the problems which words cause, and will suggest ways of controlling them so that they are not masters but servants, and the most obedient servants at that.

Spelling and spell-checking

A word has first of all to be recognized: for example, 'eleviate' is a combination of 'elevate' and 'alleviate', and it is not necessarily clear which is meant. Bad spelling not only gives a poor impression but also creates confusion and undermines confidence in the writer's technical ability. Many good, fluent and well-qualified writers have spelling problems, and the English language does little to help them.

Rules, as will be seen later in this chapter, help with punctuation but are of little use as far as spelling is concerned. A few, such as 'i' before 'e' except after 'c', as long as the sound is 'ee', work most of the time, but many rules are based on complex stress patterns or on the original Latin or Greek from which the English words are derived, or have so many exceptions that the rule is hardly worth the effort needed to learn it.

There are three categories of spelling problems, which need to be treated in different ways. First, there are the complex technical words which will not be found in an ordinary dictionary or in the computer's word files. These need to be checked in a reliable source (technical dictionary or a major textbook or journal in the field), and, if they are to be used frequently, added to the computer's list. They should always be double-checked, as it is only too easy to add an incorrectly spelt word and so to cause confusion to a wide range of users.

Second, there is the enormous number of ordinary words which are clearly out to get the writer. These gremlin words are notorious, 'necessary' being probably the most famous and 'supersede' perhaps the most tricky. Some fortunate people are born good spellers, and have no difficulty with these words, while others will rely heavily on a dictionary, whether in book form or computerized. While the computer spell-check is invaluable in picking up 'nonsense' spelling, it will not, of course, recognize the wrong form of word ('their' instead of 'there'), or a mis-spelling which creates a different word. A small poem, An Ode to the Computer Spell-check, makes the point—and illustrates the dangers of relying too heavily on the computer's knowledge. Every word would be acceptable to a machine, but most are recognizably wrong to a human being:

Eye wood rather sea a flour inn a would
Than on sail beside the rode.
Wood knot ewe?
Oar yew?

Use the spell-check with care, and keep handy a printed dictionary which gives definitions as well as the correct spellings!

The third category of difficult words consists of newcomers, which often inhabit a grey twilight zone until the language has decided how to deal with them. At first, these words frequently consist of two old words hyphenated; before long, the two words will be run together as one. Online, database and workstation are examples of this tendency. Until a particular usage is established, it is best to follow the practice of learned journals on the subject, remembering that a common pattern in English is to join words together as in the examples above.

Hyphens

Hyphens are used much less frequently than in the past. 'Today' was once written 'to-day', which now seems strange, and on the whole we use hyphens only to join words which would otherwise be ambiguous: 'extra-rational' is *outside* reason; 'extra rational' might mean 'more reasonable than usual'. Sometimes the distinction of meaning is most important: 'a cross-section of staff' is quite different from 'a cross section of staff', and 'a crosssection of staff' looks silly (English dislikes to see the same letter written consecutively three times: hence 'Mrs Jones's shop' is more commonly written as 'Mrs Jones' shop').

Americanisms

Divergences between English and American usage also have to be remembered. Generally, each country understands that the other has words which are spelt in a different way, such as the American single 'l' in a word like 'traveling', or 'color' instead of the English 'colour'. Unless there is a request for a particular version, it is simplest to keep to the forms with which the writer is most familiar. A few words are probably in transition and some do not fit happily to English usage, as the American addition of 'wise' as a suffix ('pricewise'). 'Alright' may be acceptable in the United States, but only 'all right' is correct in England. No doubt other words will cross the Atlantic, or sink in mid-ocean, in the future. It is worth remembering that computer dictionaries tend to have American spellings, which may cause problems of consistency; the English forms can, of course, be added.

Word pairs

Gremlin words often come in pairs, linked by their sound or by their appearance. 'Principle' and 'principal' sound very similar but have different meanings (principles are to do with morality; the principal is the boss), while 'deprecate' and 'depreciate' are lookalikes, but should not be confused (to deprecate is to deplore something, while depreciate is what secondhand cars do). Some pairs have similar derivations but have moved far apart: 'uninterested' simply means having no interest in, while 'disinterested' means impartial. A magistrate may safely be the latter, but never the former, which suggests boredom. Words occasionally change spelling when they are used for different parts of speech: we may advise a course of action but we give advice, and a licence to kill does not mean that we are necessarily licensed to do so. Nor should we devise a murderous device. A list of commonly confused and mis-used words can be found at the end of this chapter, with examples of their correct use.

Choosing the right word

Some words mean too little and others too much. 'Empty' words are frequently used to occupy space without the need for thought: 'quite satisfactory' is not noticeably different from 'satisfactory', and 'absolutely fatal' suggests degrees of death in the same way that 'totally complete' suggests that some things are more complete than others. The effect of using 'quite', 'fairly', 'rather' and other such empty words is to suggest that the writer lacks confidence in the material, which should never be true of report writers.

On the other hand, a common affliction is the desire to impress by using inflated language, words which are too big for their context. 'Advise' meaning 'tell' or 'inform' should be kept distinct from 'advise' meaning 'give advice', and a 'locality' is no more than a 'place'. Sometimes whole phrases mean the same as a single word: 'we are in a position to undertake' probably means 'we can'. It is always a temptation to describe a problem as a crisis, but if we do, there is no word left for the crisis when it happens. The pompously written sentence:

> Inspection of the kitchen suggests that many items of equipment are left on when not in use and this mode of operation should be avoided

is easily ignored: a large 'SWITCH OFF' notice above the cooker has immediate impact.

Clichés

Words and phrases can lose their meaning with over-use. The most famous cliché, 'Unaccustomed as I am to public speaking', could now be used only for humorous effect and not out of humility. Letters which begin 'I am writing to inform you' state the obvious, while 'in this day and age' certainly 'leaves much to be desired' and should be 'conspicuous by its absence'.

Jargon

Closely related to the cliché is unnecessary jargon. Necessary jargon is the tool of the trade (cliché), that is, professionally used words which are acceptable to readers from the same profession, who will clearly understand the meaning. 'Geotechnics' is a pleasant word used by geologists, while most of us would probably settle for 'geological features' or some such part-equivalent; a Cartomancy Congress sounds highly scientific, but would a Fortune Tellers' Congress have the same effect? If, and the 'if' is important, the reader understands and uses the same term, then it is acceptable jargon. However, unnecessary jargon is highly infectious and much less desirable. 'Basically' is a good word if the writer means 'this is the basis of what I am writing about', but its popularity as a sentence filler is to be deplored. A 'facilitator' helps a 'situation', which sounds fine but means little. Indeed, the spread of unnecessary jargon is such that sentences can be created of 90 per cent meaninglessness:

At this present moment in time, we are experiencing an ongoing crisis situation with our *Brassica oleracea*, although in due course a substantial number will become viable and at the end of the day they will be readily available at the neighbourhood retailing outlet.

In other words, 'We've a shortage of cabbages now, but they will be in the shops soon'. ('Substantial' is a 'loaded' word: you might see my wage rise as substantial, but I probably wouldn't; it's almost as bad as 'up to 30% off', meaning 'only 1% off, but we wish it could have been 29%!)

'Loaded' words

'Loaded' words have meanings which are sensed by the reader, as well as intellectually understood dictionary meanings. To be interviewed can be pleasurably exciting (a new job, promotion), but to be questioned suggests trouble with the police. We may attempt to make a point forcefully, but sound aggressive to others. A crowd is described as a mob, and there has clearly been trouble. The choice of one word rather than another suggests overtones of meaning to the reader, and the choice has to be made with subtle skill (or deviousness, depending how you look at it) in order to make sure that the effect is the one desired. As is so often true in using English, awareness is the key. The more we notice words and how other people use them, the more we become responsive to the power of words and the more skilful our own usage will become.

New words

One final word about words. As technology advances, old words are used in new ways (*data*, a plural word, has become the equivalent of a singular collective noun), new words are invented (*breathalysers* joined the English language in about 1960), and established words take on new, additional meanings and variant spellings (*disc, disk*, 'flat circular plate such as a coin', is also a gramophone record or a computer storage device).

While changes are inevitable in any living language, the development of 'pseudo-words' is disturbing to the reader and does nothing to increase comprehension. Words may be joined together to form a hybrid which is not helpful: are 'socio-economic considerations' the same as 'social and economic', or is the social aspect subordinate to the economic, or, indeed, vice versa? Other 'pseudo-words' develop within particular industries. The construction industry has learnt to live with 'buildability', but 'constructionability' is ugly and unnecessary. We may converse by telephone more simply than 'telephonically'. 'Skeletonize' allows scope for the imagination: perhaps 'skeletonization' is the opposite of 'survivability'.

The previous paragraph is not a joke. All the words given have appeared in technical reports, and no doubt there are many others. They have no historical, literary or musical virtues, and, what is more, they make the reader laugh, or perhaps despair.

Sentences

Words do not only try to trap the writer in an individual capacity. They join together and swarm like locusts, terrifying the beholder and causing devastation and barrenness of meaning. Short sentences are easily controlled. Other sentences, containing more detailed information and being more complex in form, make greater demands on writer and reader alike. It has been known, however, for words to join together in large numbers, describing, qualifying and modifying one another, linked by words of humbler nature to form phrases and clauses of greater or lesser complexity which in turn are joined, in the nature of the sentence itself, in order to form a whole which is satisfying and intelligible to the reader.

Sentence length

The reader of this book will have just seen that while short sentences are easy to understand, enormous sentences are extremely difficult. If the report writer wishes to help the reader, sentence length must be tightly controlled, and the purpose of each sentence established.

A series of very short sentences, of perhaps fewer than ten words, is jerky and awkward, sounding like a small child's learn-to-read book. In a report this can be useful, as a series of facts will be easily assimilated in a list composed of short sentences. As the sentence grows in length, so the rate of reading will be slowed down and the reader forced to reflect on the ideas presented. An 'average' sentence has about 17 to 20 words; if the intention is to help the reader to consider and evaluate various possible interpretations of data, sentences of 20 to 25 words will have the right effect. As soon as a sentence exceeds 30 words, there is a danger that the reader will have too much to assimilate without the breathing space of a full stop. Obviously, the complexity or otherwise of the material will affect the length of the sentences, but variety helps the flow of the reading and improves the style. Some long, some middle-sized and some short sentences produce the most readable material, but no sentence should be too long, or allowed to get out of control.

Sentence control

The problem of sentence control is best seen in examples, taken from real-life reports, of how words can escape from the writer's head to create confusion. A sentence must make complete sense within itself. The following is not a sentence:

> To ensure the system will not be adversely affected by periods of bad weather, or sudden failure in the mains supply, when good communications during these sometimes chaotic conditions will be essential.

To ensure the system works—what must be done? The sentence has no grammatical end, and cannot therefore make sense. We may guess at what the writer intended: the system must perform satisfactorily even under extreme conditions. How this is to be ensured, we are not told. Many sentences simply contain too much information:

> Predominantly a peak heating system such as ceiling heating which is designed for continuous operation throughout the heating season, is generally used by tenants intermittently, this gives rise to complaints of cold feet and legs, high running cost and poor value for money.

Apart from the unintentional humour of the juxtaposition of cold feet and legs and high running cost, and some grammatical oddities such as 'system' when the plural 'systems' must be intended, there is one basic problem. The sentence is too long. Its perpetrator might usefully have sat back and looked at the separate pieces of information available.

1. Ceiling heating is a form of peak heating system.

2. Any peak heating system is designed to be used continuously.

3. The limits to continuous use are decided by the weather (or the calendar, or the landlord).

4. Generally, tenants use the system intermittently.

5. The tenants (?) complain of cold feet and legs.

6. The running cost is high.

7. The system appears to be poor value for money.

There are four sections of information here. First is the explanation of the system and its intended use, second is the way in which it is nevertheless being used, third, is the result of that usage from the tenants' point of view, and fourth is the economic factor. These sections immediately suggest sentences, each being a clearly defined package of information which will make complete sense in itself. So:

1. Ceiling heating, like any peak heating system, is intended to be used continuously during the period October to May (or during the winter).

2. Tenants are at present using the system intermittently.

3. As a result, the tenants complain of the apparent inefficiency of the system. They suffer from cold feet and legs.

4. The running cost of using the system in this way in high, and the landlord and the tenants are getting poor value for money.

Four sentences will make a tidy paragraph (see next section). If the report is written for the tenants, sentence 3 might be used first, while if it is written for the landlord, sentence 4 will attract immediate attention. So:

As the ceiling heating is operated at present, the running cost is high and the system appears to be poor value for money. However, as with all peak heating systems, it was designed for continuous operation throughout the winter. At present, it is used intermittently by the tenants and is therefore working inefficiently. As a result, we are receiving complaints from the tenants about cold feet and legs.

The ordering of ideas is now clear, and the paragraph is much easier to read than the original. Nevertheless, the equal length of the sentences makes for a certain monotony, and the paragraph might be improved with a little variety:

As the ceiling heating is operated at present, the running cost is high and the system appears to represent poor value for money. However, as with all peak heating systems, it was designed for continuous operation during the winter. Tenants often use it intermittently and, inevitably, they complain of the cold.

While admittedly a certain licence has been taken with the material of the original attempt, the picture is clear: wrong use of system, unhappy tenants, waste of money.

The process of sentence construction has now been analysed. First of all, the writer must decide exactly what has to be said, and, at least mentally, list the various points. Each point can be seen as a separate sentence, and the sentences arranged logically, or according to the impact on the reader. Then the sentences can be written in order, but adapted to give variety of length and structure. The process is not as lengthy as it sounds, and in any case it must be faster and cheaper than a series of letters or telephone calls needed in order to extract meaning from confused writing.

It is often helpful to read a long sentence out loud. If the report writer runs out of breath before the end, the sentence is probably too long. Where the voice pauses naturally, a comma is usually appropriate, and if the *writer* is confused at the end, then the recipients of the report certainly will be. The awkwardness of the following real-life sentence is clear as soon as it is heard:

Further investigation such as taking core samples to ascertain thickness and the degree of corosion (*sic*) of the brick mortar jointing, might be necessary to have carried out.

The next step for the report writer is to ask what words would be *spoken* if this were part of a conversation. It would probably be something like this:

> Well, we might have to look further, you know, perhaps take some core samples. We'd want to know about the brick mortar jointing, how thick it is, and how far it's corroded.

The original sentence is now two sentences, and the language has been simplified. It has become too chatty for a formal report, and so a balance must be found:

> It might be necessary to take core samples (this stage *is* 'further investigation') to find the thickness and degree of corrosion of the brick mortar jointing.

Twenty-seven words have been reduced to 21, and the sentence says what it means in a straightforward way. 'Back to front' sentences are particularly irritating, as the reader has to get to the end in order to understand the message:

> Based on the fact that the terms and conditions of the Original Order prevail on the Amendments then these items do not fall into the Liquidated Damages period.

The writer of the sentence probably wanted to impress (hence the number of capital letters), but the second part of the sentence carries the essentials, and it should be moved to the start:

> These items do not fall into the Liquidated Damages period since the terms and conditions of the Original Order prevail over the Amendments.

Punctuation

Much of the difficulty of sentence construction comes, as has been seen, from a lack of punctuation, or from inaccurate punctuation. A good rule-of-thumb guide is to read aloud, as a full stop is intended to allow the reader time to assimilate what has gone before and prepare for what is to come, while a comma is a pause for (mental) breath. Commas also show how the sentence should be read:

1. However difficulties might arise, we will be able to solve them.

2. However difficulties might arise, although we will be able to solve them.

3. However, difficulties might arise although we will be able to solve them.

Sentences 1 and 3 are clear, and the reader knows how to understand them; Sentence 2 is not clear, because the reader cannot guess until he reaches 'although', halfway through the sentence, whether 'however' is a comment on the situation or whether it means 'in whatever way', Indeed, the meaning of a sentence may change radically with the punctuation:

> The engines, which have been stripped down, are now in working order.
> The engines which have been stripped down are now in working order.

The first sentence, of course, refers to *all* engines, while the second only to those which have been stripped down. Carried to extremes, confused punctuation can lead to very odd sentences, as in this real-life example:

> We have not included dampers unfortunately, not sufficient information available to enable accurate sizing however, as in the case of valves, we have provided motors and actuators.

Perhaps the writer intended:

> Unfortunately, we have not included dampers as we have insufficient information for accurate sizing. However, as in the case of valves, we have provided motors and actuators.

The reader, unfortunately, has to guess at the meaning. Punctuation is, however, less of a problem to the would-be writer than is spelling. Most punctuation obeys clear rules with rare exceptions, and it is worth learning at least the most helpful rules, which are probably to do with full stops and commas. The Bibliography (page 111) recommends books which will help and which have good examples; in this book we can point out only a few of the most common errors.

A sentence must, as we have said, make complete sense in itself, and it must contain a main verb:

> This being a delicate situation, if our clients decide to cut back on the project although at this stage our involvement is not great.

This is not a sentence, as there are three subordinate sections, that is, a part-verb 'being', a conditional clause 'if you decide', and a modifying clause 'although ... is not great'. One of these must be made into a main verb if the words are to form a sensible sentence, and the most likely is that 'being' will become 'will be'. Again, if the original is read aloud, it can be heard not to make complete sense.

Apostrophes

Probably more trouble is caused by the little word 'its' (or 'it's') than any other of comparable size in the English language. Apostrophes, it is often said, are an endangered species. Unfortunately their survival is often important to the meaning of a sentence. In the case of 'its', the difficulty is easily overcome: if 'it is' or 'it has' is meant, then there is an apostrophe, and if it isn't, there isn't. (So: 'I've looked at the car and *it's* obvious that *its* tyres are reaching the legal limit.')

There are only two uses of the apostrophe: to show where a letter is missed out (the 'i' in 'it is'), and to show possession. As the former use is inappropriate to a report ('it is' should always be written in full), only the possessive is likely to cause trouble. Usually, the sense will be clear whether the apostrophe is present or not, but sometimes the apostrophe is essential to the meaning:

We have had many years of experience in dealing with our clients problems.

Many years with *one* client ('client's problems') or various clients ('clients' problems')? If we are interested in the experience, we will certainly want to know whether it is broadly-based or not. For this reason, the apostrophe is needed, and such cases should ensure that, in formal writing at least, the apostrophe is kept alive.

Colons and semi-colons

The distinction between the colon and the semi-colon often bewilders the report writer. A colon is used to introduce a list of individual items, as in the following:

In order to conduct this experiment, we need the following equipment:
  test tubes
  retort
  Bunsen burners
  reagents
  litmus paper

It also introduces a quotation or example, as in the previous paragraph ('as in the following:'), or a list of points which have to be considered. So:

In reading the report, we noted:

1. that the contents list did not always agree with the contents provided;

2. that the standard of writing was not consistent with the gravity of the problem investigated;

3. that the binding broke after a few handlings, and pages fell out.

In this example, the precise rules for introducing the list have been followed: colon followed by continuations of the introductory sentence, each ending with a semi-colon, until the final point which concludes the sentence and ends with a full stop. However, in the list of items of equipment, given above, semi-colons would be cumbersome and have been omitted. If individual points are too long and in themselves contain complete sentences, then once more the system is broken:

The observations noted when the report was read are listed below.

1. The contents list did not always agree with the contents provided. A section on the use of diagrams is listed but could not be found, and the page references are wrong in at least three instances. Appendix C appears, strangely, before Appendix B.

Clearly, it would be peculiar to have a semi-colon after 'Appendix B', and the second point must start as a new sentence.

A semi-colon is almost as strong a pause as a full stop. It connects two complete sentences which are so strongly related in meaning (often contrast or paradox) that the writer wants to stress the link without joining them into one:

Old steam engines are to be seen, paint fresh and brass gleaming; the modern inter-city train may be faster, but it is dingy and uncared-for beside its forebear.

The contrast is more pointed because of the semi-colon. This is an elegant piece of punctuation and reads well, but too many semi-colons become heavy and lose their effect. Occasionally and judicially used, they are effective.

Abbreviations and acronyms

Generally speaking, less punctuation is used in abbreviations nowadays than in the past. Most people will type 'etc' or 'eg' without full stops (much as punctuation has largely disappeared from addresses), and names of countries (UK, USA) have also lost their punctuation.

Acronyms (abbreviations which have become independent words, such as NATO or NALGO), have no punctuation, though the writer must always check the official form of the word, especially with regard to capital or lower case letters. Names of companies should be similarly checked on a letterhead or other reputable source; some have familiarly abbreviated names, such as Boots, and some use internal punctuation while others do not, for instance WH Smith.

Grammar

This is not a grammar textbook (see Bibliography), and only a few common grammatical problems can be looked at. However, the writer of good reports will be constantly aware of the need for accurate grammar, and will notice, too, how helpful to the reader is a well-constructed, grammatically-correct report.

Problems can occur when a sentence changes construction mid-way:

> Having conducted the experiment and being certain that my results were accurate and therefore I decided to write the article and see my efforts in print.

'Having conducted ... I decided', or 'I had conducted the experiment ... and therefore' would each be correct, but the two constructions should not be confused.

Unrelated participles

Unrelated participles are a common source of entertainment inappropriate to a report. In the previous example, 'Having conducted ...' leads to the subject 'I', and it is clear that 'I' have conducted the experiment. 'Having' is a participle, not a complete verb, and it has to wait until after the comma for its subject to appear; that subject is usually the subject also of the main verb:

Having conducted the experiment ...   I decided to write ...

↖   ↖   ↖

(Participle)   (Subject) (main verb)

If the apparent subject of the participle is not the real subject, the result can be very odd:

Driving as fast as possible, the bridge came into view within an hour.

'Driving' is the participle and 'bridge' *appears* to be its subject and indeed *is* the subject of the main verb 'came', but it is unlikely that the bridge drove anywhere, quickly or otherwise. A particularly entertaining real-life example of the unrelated participle problem appears in a guide book:

Having been thoroughly cleaned and renovated, visitors to the Cathedral will be impressed ...

Poor visitors!

Singular/plural confusion

The confusion of singular and plural often results from a failure to identify correctly the subject of the sentence:

There is a wide range of materials available, which allow us to choose the most suitable for our purpose.

The subject of 'is available' is 'wide range', which is singular; the second part of the sentence must therefore begin 'which allows us ...'. The problem word, of course, is 'materials', which is plural and which intervenes between subject and verb, and which is mistakenly thought of as the subject. 'Each' tends to create singular/plural confusion:

Each of the engineers concerned have written a report.

This is wrong, as the subject of 'have written' is 'each' (which means 'each one' and is therefore singular) and not 'engineers'. So:

Each of the engineers concerned has written a report.

Misuse of 'each' can again sometimes be entertaining:

There is a stretch of water between each bridge

presumably means that the river has flooded and each bridge is awash, and highly dangerous! The sentence makes sense if 'and the next' is added, as water between two *bridges* is not uncommon.

Unnecessary repetition

Two common errors will complete this brief survey of grammatical problems. 'The reason is because' is unnecessary repetition, as clearly 'the reason' *is* 'because'. It is easily and wrongly written:

The reason that the project was a failure and had to be abandoned was because technical collaboration between the two countries concerned became impossible.

The writer has forgotten that he began with 'the reason', and so has felt the need to use 'because'. Correctly, the sentence could be either 'The reason that the project ... was that technical collaboration ...' or 'The project was a failure ... because technical collaboration ...', but not both at the same time.

'Only'

A peculiarly treacherous word in spite of its size is 'only'. It must be placed as closely as possible to the word or words it refers to, as its position will affect the meaning of the sentence. If the sentence reads:

The financial manager offered me twice the salary I am currently receiving if I worked abroad for a year

then we should certainly want to know, if we received such an offer, where 'only' might be placed. There are many possible positions, and if the sentence is read with each 'only' in turn, it is obvious that the offer becomes more or less attractive:

(Only) the financial manager offered (only) me (only) twice the salary (only) I am currently receiving if (only) I worked abroad for a year (only).

Worked example of confused expression

An example from a genuine report illustrates some of the problems of inaccurate writing:

> The material certificates pages 5, 6 and 7 as your client has observed have dates 1983, 1984 and 1978 respectively, the latter is the vibrating spool for the density meter this is a very special alloy and can only be brought (*sic*) in bulk, and as such small quantities of material are used in each meter this certificate is relevant to the equipment supplied.

The problems are listed below.

1.	material certificates pages:	an apostrophe needed on 'certificates', but the phrase would read much more easily as 'pages 5, 6 and 7 of the material certificates'.
2.	as your client has observed:	easier to read if it is placed between commas. It is a comment on the rest, and we would read it aloud with a pause before and after.
3.	respectively:	this is the end of the first section of information, and should be followed by a full stop and a new sentence.
4.	the latter:	'the latter' describes the second of two items (the other being 'the former'). As there are three pages and dates mentioned, it is not clear whether 'the latter' refers to pages 6 and 7, or just page 7.
5.	is the vibrating spool:	can a page (or indeed a date) be a vibrating spool? 'Is' presumably means 'refers to'.
6.	density meter:	this is the end of the second section of information, and so should be followed by a full stop and a new sentence.
7.	is (a very special alloy):	'is' would be clearer as 'is made of'.
8.	very:	adds nothing to the meaning.
9.	brought:	a typing error: read 'bought' (and see Chapter 6).
10.	only:	a 'danger' word, as described above. Almost certainly, the writer meant that the alloy can be bought *only* in bulk, and not 'only bought'.

11. bulk:	this is the end of the third section of information, and so should be followed by a full stop and a new sentence.
12. as such:	there is nothing wrong with this expression, but we read it in two ways: 'as such small quantities', or 'as such ...'. If the ambiguity makes the reader go back and reread the phrase, it would be better to write 'since'.
13. each meter:	should be followed by a comma for ease of reading.

The original passage may now be rewritten as follows:

> Pages 5, 6 and 7 of the material certificates, as your client has observed, have dates 1983, 1984 and 1978 respectively. The last of these refers to the vibrating spool for the density meter, which is made of a special alloy obtainable only in bulk purchase. Since each meter takes only a very small quantity of material, this certificate remains relevant to the equipment supplied.

We may query whether it is worth mentioning pages 6 and 7, or the dates 1983 and 1984, at all. The reader wants to know that the certificate, in spite of its date, is still valid, and it might be wise to put that first:

> Page 7 of the material certificate, as your client has observed, is dated 1978. It is still valid. The alloy referred to is bought in bulk, and only a small quantity is used in each meter.

In rewriting this piece, we have assumed that the client had queried the early date (1978) of one of the certificates, and the report was intended to answer the query. No writing, however, should depend upon the reader's assumption of meaning, as the consequences of a mistaken assumption are too serious. Inaccurate or ambiguous expression costs money.

Paragraphs

If words can be gremlins and sentences locusts, there is no adequate term for the monstrous paragraphs which often appear in reports. It is depressing to turn over a page and to be faced with great chunks of print, with no opportunity for a pause or a feeling of satisfaction that one section at least has been read and understood. A paragraph usually deals with one aspect of the subject under discussion, and is as long as is necessary for that aspect to be covered adequately. At the same time, the average of three paragraphs to a page looks satisfactory and manageable to the reader. A compromise has to be reached. Reports tend to have shorter paragraphs than books or articles, and five or six paragraphs to a page is not unusual. The dictates of the subject matter and the ease of the reader are, as usual, the criteria on which decisions are based. For example, the following paragraph is difficult to assimilate because of the number of facts included (the facts are based on information provided by courtesy of the Motor Industry Information Service, which is operated by the Society of Motor Manufacturers and Traders):

> More than 25 million people in Britain hold a driving licence. 8 out of every 10 tons of freight go by road. Each freight vehicle carries 3 times as much as its equivalent 30 years ago. 1% of passenger journeys are by bicycle. Britain has fewer motorways than France or Germany. More than half the British working population goes to work by car. The motor industry provides over a million jobs. 84% of passenger journeys are by private transport. Motor exports are second only to oil. More than 20 000 dealers and garages sell and service motor vehicles in Britain. Car ownership per thousand of population grew from 108 to 295 in Britain between 1960 and 1983.

The sentences are grammatically correct, although of a boringly uniform length, but the total effect of the paragraph is confusion. The material must be grouped according to aspect of the subject, each aspect providing a new paragraph. Aspects included are:

people and cars
motorways
freight carriage
exports
motor industry employment
bicycles

Some of these aspects, for instance people and cars/bicycles, are linked by contrast. Exports is too small an aspect to stand by itself, and it could provide a useful comment on the size of the motor industry (although a case could be made for putting it elsewhere). If the ideas are grouped in this way, the following passage might result:

More than 25 million people in Britain hold a driving licence, and over half the working population goes to work by car. Indeed, 84% of passenger journeys are by private transport, of which only 1% is by bicycle. It is not surprising to learn that in Britain car ownership per thousand of population rose from 108 to 295 between 1960 and 1983.

In spite of the fact that Britain has fewer motorways than either France or Germany, freight carriage is largely by road, eight out of every ten tons being transported in this way. Nevertheless, the efficiency of the system is shown by the fact that each freight transporter carries three times as much as its equivalent did 30 years ago.

The motor industry is a major employer, providing over a million jobs. More than 20 000 dealers and garages sell and service motor vehicles in Britain. Motor exports are second only to oil.

These three paragraphs are short, clearly defined in material, and much more easily read and assimilated than the original. Careful paragraphing is important in producing reader goodwill.

Style

So far in this chapter, we have looked at some of the constituent parts of English usage: words, sentences, punctuation, grammar and paragraphs. If all these are used accurately, with the convenience of the reader in mind, the report will be acceptable and easy to use. It will not necessarily be a pleasure to read. Style is difficult to define, but it is essentially the manner of writing as opposed to the material. The first version of the motor transport facts given above was accurately written, but bad style; the revised version was accurate and much better in style, helpful to the reader and achieving a certain fluency. Good style comes largely from practice, not just practice at writing but also practice at criticism, at considering the good and bad points of reports, articles and books. The good ones should then be tried out, and the bad ones consciously avoided.

Levels of formality

Reports are formal documents. They do not have to be pompous in style, or literary, but they do have to conform to a standard of business writing which is acceptable to the recipient. Within the formality, then, there are variations. A short note, sent to update the information a colleague already has, is comparatively informal. It must be grammatically correct to avoid ambiguity, but it may well use abbreviations ('we've had a look at the machinery, and in the light of what we found last time, you'll be pleased to know that ...'). Such a message will probably be transmitted in the form of a memo.

An in-company report which is intended for a number of people, including those higher in the hierarchy than the writer, is more formal. It does not use abbreviations, and should not contain slang, and it will be 'politically' acceptable, that is, it uses tact in the expression. 'We're getting fed up with the number of hold-ups in getting spares so we can't ever seem to get a move on' is the spoken word; 'We're always being held up for spares and it's causing frustration' might be the memo version; 'The lack of adequate spares provision is delaying output' would appear in the report. The slang 'fed up with' and the personal irritation have disappeared, while a clear objective statement of the problem has taken their place.

The level of formality is sometimes the subject of company policy. A report may be produced by 'me' or 'us' or 'the company', and the right usage is that demanded by the company's arbiters of taste. The choice is often between 'We recommended' and 'It is recommended that': the former is shorter and more direct, but the latter may be preferred because of its formality and its distancing of the individual from a company statement. Sometimes policy dictates that 'I' or 'we' is acceptable for internal reports but not for reports going outside the company. While this is obviously a decision for the individual organization, the report writer must be aware of the danger of changing a personal statement into an impersonal one: 'I cannot accept the idea' is different from 'The idea cannot be accepted', and it is usually true that the impersonal will be more wide-ranging than the personal: 'I suspect that ...' is more limited than 'A suspicion may arise that ...' Whatever the decision about 'I' or 'we', readers should never be directly addressed as 'you', or asked direct questions which they are unlikely to answer. In this respect, a written report differs from a spoken presentation.

Writing in the active voice ('I recommend') is, as has been pointed out above, shorter and more direct than the passive ('It is recommended'). If there is a choice, the active is preferable for these reasons, as in this example:

We checked our figures and found the projected expenditure acceptable. (active: 10 words)
The figures were checked and the projected expenditure was found to be acceptable. (passive: 13 words)

Abstract v. concrete words

Abstract words can be in themselves a barrier to understanding. The clearest, easiest writing is made up of precise, 'concrete' terms which the reader can visualize. In the following sentence, the abstract words: flexibility, keynote, policy, possibly, basis, intervals, variety and concentration, produce a dazed reaction in the reader, so that the simple message is lost:

> Flexibility is the keynote to our company policy, and therefore where the possibility exists, workers are redirected on a rota basis at regular intervals to ensure variety and thereby aid concentration.

If the abstract terms can be exchanged for precise, literal words, the sentence is immediately easier to understand:

> This company believes that workers can concentrate more easily if they have a change of job every week or so. Where it is possible, therefore, a rota will be produced to give everyone variety in his or her work.

'Variety' is the only abstract idea remaining, and in the context of the two shorter sentences, its meaning is clear.

Split infinitives

Good style is partly the result of logical thought. The old problem of the split infinitive ('to boldly go') shows an illogical approach to sentence structure.

> After the alterations, it was possible to more easily move round the workshop.

The meaning is clear, but the infinitive ('to move') is one unit of the sentence, and the adverbial phrase ('more easily') refers to the whole idea of 'to move'. The sentence units should be brought together:

> After the alterations, it was possible to move round the workshop more easily.

Nevertheless, English is a living language much less bound by rules and regulations than many other European languages, and one of its strengths is that if you know the rules, you are allowed to break them. Breaking the rules should be rare and carried out for an important reason, but with these provisos, the infinitive may be split:

It is essential to thoroughly disinfect the equipment.

Emphasis is thrown on the offending word 'thoroughly', which is presumably intended to carry great force, and, in such a case, the breaking of the rule is justified. It follows, however, that such a sentence must be very unusual or the emphasis will be lost.

Mixed metaphors

The mixed metaphor has no place in reports or any other writing, and it too follows from illogicality. Earlier in this chapter, we wrote of gremlin words and locust sentences: such writing would be inappropriate to a formal, objective report, but perhaps brightens a book *about* reports. If we had written:

A gathering of gremlin words produces a locust sentence

we should have been guilty of mixing metaphors: whatever the collective noun for gremlins is, it does not produce locusts! One despairing colleague was heard to say of another:

Every time he gets a bee in his bonnet he goes into it like a bull in a china shop

which mixes metaphors which are in themselves clichés, and so offends twice.

Such writing interrupts the reader, as do slang and jargon, because it draws attention to itself and away from the information to be conveyed. Abbreviations can have the same effect when they are inappropriately used. 'E.g.' and 'i.e.' are acceptable where a list of facts is given, or a number of examples or explanations, but in the middle of a piece of continuous prose the words should be written in full. 'For example, or 'that is' take very little longer to write, but allow the reader to move on without interference to the flow of the reading. Repetitive sentence or paragraph starts will also tend to distract the reader, and it is usually easy to avoid the problem by turning one sentence round. Two sentences in a paragraph or two paragraphs on a page may start with the same few words, but more than that will draw attention to an awkwardness of style.

Logical links

On the other hand, linking words or phrases help the reader, not only improving the flow of the style but also guiding the reader in the approach to what follows. 'On the other hand', at the beginning of this paragraph, implied that what follows is a contrast to what has gone before (helping the flow rather than hindering it); 'in contrast' has a similar effect, while 'at the same time' suggests holding two points in tension, as does 'bearing in mind . . .'. Such words or phrases must be used carefully: 'therefore' must introduce the logical consequence of what has just been written, while 'nevertheless' tells readers to assume that in spite of what they have just read, there is another point to be considered. Linking words tell readers how to order their minds for the next sentence or paragraph and, although that ordering will usually be subconscious, it is important in encouraging them to read on.

The ability to write well is, as we said at the beginning of this chapter, a skill which results from an awareness of meaning and implication, and from hard work. Most writers, however experienced, feel a moment of panic when they are faced with a blank sheet of paper and the necessity of writing on it. 'Get started' is good advice, and in the case of report writing the start may be made at any point in the document. Often, the main body of the report with its factual evidence is a good place to begin: even if only one short section is available, write that section first. It may need revision later, but at least the psychological barrier is removed. The paper is no longer blank, and the report writer has proved that he or she can produce something. This is true for all writing, even if, as in the case of this chapter and indeed of this book, the first words are Shakespeare's.

List of commonly mis-used words

Aggravate
make worse (*not* irritate)
The soreness on the runner's heel was aggravated by new running shoes.

Anticipate
pre-empt (*not* expect)
The fielder anticipated the flight of the ball accurately and so was able to catch it.

Chronic
long-lasting or **constant** (*not* serious)
Chronic illness led to depression which was not serious enough to allow the manager to take time off work.

Contemporary
at the same time as (*not* modern)
The Black Death was contemporary with, and indeed interrupted, the building of some fine fourteenth-century churches.

Disinterested
impartial, unbiased (*not* bored)
When they visited the court, they were so moved by the plight of the accused that they found it difficult to remain disinterested observers.

Enormity
severity (*not* large-size)
The enormity of the crime was such that the criminal received a life sentence.

Fortuitous
accidental (*not* fortunate)
It was fortuitous that the old enemies appeared in the area at the same time, and ominous for both of them.

Infer
deduce (*not* suggest, imply)
When the manager implied that you were much better at the job than your predecessor had been, I inferred that you would be promoted as soon as there was a vacancy.

Literally
actually (*not* metaphorically; in the example below, 'too big for his boots' refers to size, not arrogance)
The young football player had literally become too big for his boots, so his mother had to buy him a larger pair.

Pristine
fresh as if new (*not* good)

As the book had not been removed from its wrapping, it was still in pristine condition.

Problematic
dubious, unsure (*not* difficult, full of problems)
The outcome of the trial was problematic, as both defence and prosecution had convincing arguments.

Refute
rebut, prove false (*not* disagree with)
Greater knowledge and experience allowed the professor to refute the student's argument.

Regularly
at regular intervals (*not* frequently)
Haley's comet appears regularly every 76 years.

Unique
once only (*not* rare)
The first day of the new century will be a unique event in my lifetime, as I am unlikely to live to be 150 years old.

Vital
essential to life (*not* important)
The brain is a vital organ, without which the body would cease to function.

Key points in Chapter 4

- Your report must be unambiguous, grammatically correct and as easy as possible to read.

- Use a computer spell-check with care and have a dictionary available.

- Choose words which convey your meaning accurately and concisely, avoiding clichés and jargon.

- Vary the length of sentences, avoiding the over-long or over-complicated.

- Decide what you want to say and put the ideas in a logical order; check that each sentence makes complete sense by itself and adds to the meaning of the whole passage.

- Check the punctuation by reading your sentence aloud. It's helpful if its apostrophes are used correctly!

- Structure your information into well-ordered paragraphs, and avoid the depressing effect of long, solid blocks of print.

- Make sure that your report is a formal document in both format and style.

- Remember that good style is easy to read and does not draw attention to itself.

CHAPTER 5

Data presentation

Convention and familiarity · Choice of format · Positioning of diagrams ·
Titles and numbers · Photocopying · Space and shape · Conclusion

Reports are dependent for their impact on words, and the words are often supported by diagrams. 'Supported by' suggests the most appropriate function of a diagram: it does not simply replace lots of words, or repeat them, it elucidates the meaning of the text by presenting particular information in a helpful and revealing way, when words by themselves would be difficult to understand.

Car accident reports—and insurance claim forms—provide a good example of the power of a diagram. The details of the accident, the exact sequence of events, will be expressed in words. The position of the vehicles before and after the accident is best shown by a sketch—words would be inadequate. The writer has to decide, perhaps with a little prompting from the form itself, which information should most appropriately be presented in words and which in a diagram.

The same choice of presentation faces the report writer. A great deal of numerical information, or other complex detail, written in prose causes confusion, dismay and mistakes. Figures may be difficult to extract, and more time, which means also more money, will be needed for the reader to use the report material accurately. In this chapter, we will look at different ways of presenting information in a form which is easy to assimilate, that is, in diagrams, the word 'diagram' being taken to include tables, graphs and charts.

However, there is another side to such presentation. If a diagram will not clarify the situation, then it should not be used. Only relevant and helpful diagrams have their place in a report. They are an integral part of the general presentation of the material, and should never be added as an afterthought, or to break up the prose and make the page look more interesting (which, incidentally, good diagrams do, as a by-product of their main function).

Convention and familiarity

If diagrammatic information is presented in an unusual or difficult format, it becomes a problem for the reader who, understandably, will ignore or reject it unless it is essential to the comprehension. If it is essential, the reader will struggle with and be irritated by it. On the principle of trying to gain reader goodwill, it is obviously important to avoid breaking the conventions with which the reader is familiar. Familiarity, it might be said, breeds assent, and the reader will readily accept and use a convention which is recognizable. Diagrams which break with convention take longer to understand, and result in more mistakes. Clearly, it is in the writer's interest to produce a diagram which is easy to read and assimilate and which is comparatively error-free.

Sometimes, readers will convert information to a familiar format. People who recognise 75°F as indication of a fine day may not respond so cheerfully to 24°C. They may, if they know the formula, set about multiplying by 9 and dividing by 5 and adding 32 in order to get a familiar reading. Information should, whenever possible, be presented in the format with which readers are familiar and which they wish to use. As usual with report writing, identifying the readership is important, and in the case of a varied readership it may well be appropriate to offer two versions of the same information, for example, metric measurements could be followed by their imperial equivalents in brackets.

Convention is important not only in presenting figures, but also in the use of signs, symbols and abbreviations. The most common and useful conventions are contained in British Standards and International Standards, and these should be followed whenever possible. Many company libraries have the British Standards relevant to employees, and libraries in further and higher education institutions also have sets of Standards (although not always complete sets), which are updated regularly by the staff. If the report writer is in doubt, it is always worth checking the Standard convention. Numbers in themselves must follow conventional use, and it is recommended that arabic numbers are always used, and roman numerals avoided, as the latter are too easy to confuse. Page numbers, numbered lists and so on should all use arabic numbers.

Dates, especially important in report writing (see Chapter 3), can be confusing if they are given in numerical form. Is 2.7.85 the second of July 1985 or the seventh of February 1985? Unless the convention used is made very clear, perhaps by columns headed D/M/Y, then the month must be written out in word form. In a formal report, it would be inappropriate to abbreviate the month to three letters, or to miss the first two numbers of the year: the acceptable form is 2 July 1985 (or, of course, 7 February 1985).

Choice of format

Data presented in a report must be in the most suitable format for the information and for the reader. Four common formats are used: tables, bar charts, pie charts and graphs. Each will be considered in turn in the next part of this chapter, with its usage first, followed by the conventions of the particular form.

Many report writers have access to computer graphics packages which readily produce a variety of diagrams from a set of data. However, writers still have the task of selecting the most suitable format.

Tables

Tables are probably the most common form of diagram in a report. They are used when there is a great deal of accurate information to be conveyed. Frequently this information is numerical, although it can also be verbal, for instance test results showing various properties of materials. The report writer must, as in every aspect of report production, consider the needs of the report reader or user, who may not want or be capable of handling all the detail available, and would much prefer numbers to be rounded off to the appropriate values. If the reader needs seven decimal places, then of course they must be given if at all possible, but if the writer has seven decimal places and the reader will be satisfied with one, then one is the correct number. More would only confuse the reader, and make the table more difficult to use. Of course it is tempting to give all the information available, especially if it has been particularly difficult to obtain, but if it is not required, it must not be included. An over-complex table will be time-consuming for the user, who might make mistakes in using it, although at the same time it must be remembered that the reader will also be irritated if more detail is needed than the table shows. The best advice is, as usual, to know the reader and to present the data appropriately.

When checking a list of equipment, we all find it much harder to scan along a row than down a column. For example, we might note down the basic requirements for a holiday under canvas as: canvas outer, inner compartments, groundsheet, pegs, mallet, guy ropes, poles, curtains and runners, trims, repair kits, storm pole, spares and clips. It is also useful to have chairs, table, cooker and stand, sleeping bags, airbeds, crockery, cutlery, pans, cleaning equipment and cold box.

As a list, the above is cumbersome and difficult to mark off. We should not find it a helpful checklist. However, as soon as the items are written in a vertical column, we have a list we can use easily and quickly:

Canvas outer
Inner compartments
Groundsheet
Pegs
Mallet
Guy ropes
Poles
Curtains and runners
Trims
Repair kit
Storm pole
Spares
Clips

and a secondary list of desirable items can then follow. Campers can also use this list as a check by counting the number of items, in this case an unlucky 13, which is difficult to do if they are listed across the page. Most writers creating a list will automatically choose a vertical format.

This convention is important when the report writer is creating a table of information. Details which are to be scanned should be presented vertically, while related items should be presented horizontally. The direction of scan is from top to bottom and the direction for reading horizontally (at least in the Western world) is from left to right. For example, a scientist interested in the properties of a particular material would need to scan down a list of materials to the one which was required and then work horizontally along the row to read the properties. Tables which do not adhere to this format are confusing and difficult to use.

Space is the ally of diagram-makers, and especially of those who produce tables. Report readers do not enjoy being made to walk across pages with their fingers in order to make both column and row meet: it looks childish and it can easily lead to a mistake. Space is the answer. If the vertical list is broken by space after every five, or at most seven, items, then it is not difficult to identify the particular item needed. The smaller the chance of the reader's eye slipping from a line in a table, the smaller is the chance of incorrect information being extracted.

Vertical space helps in the same way. A vertical line breaks up the information on the horizontal line, and unless this is necessary for the material to be understood, it should be avoided. Generally, vertical space is more helpful. Horizontal lines may be ruled under headings to separate them from the data, and could be ruled above and below totals on the bottom line, or above and below the table to separate it from the text, but horizontal lines between items in the vertical list are unnecessary, and distract the reader's eyes from the information.

Each column of a table should have a clear, succinct heading, which precisely indicates the information below. Headings should not be centred on a column, but aligned with the left-hand edge of the column while numbers should be aligned under the decimal point, that is, hundreds under hundreds and tens under tens. Column headings should include, where appropriate, the units of measurements and powers of ten, for instance, to express millions, thousands and thousandths. Such abbreviations are common in the headings of financial tables.

Figure 5.1, Tabulated data, is an illustration of a well-presented table not from a report but from a book of statistical tables in which, unusually, numbers and titles are more appropriately placed above than below the diagrams. Its desirable qualities are listed below.

2.2 Age distribution of estimated population at 30 June 1984

Thousands

| | Home Population | | | | | | | | | | |
| | United Kingdom[1] | | | England and Wales | | Wales | | Scotland[1] | | Northern Ireland | |
	Persons	Males	Females	Males	Females	Males	Females	Males	Females	Males	Females
All ages	56 376.8	27 430.2	28 946.6	24 244.2	25 519.4	1 361.0	1 446.2	2 485.0	2 665.4	772.5	806.0
0–14	11 170.2	5 733.9	5 436.4	4 917.2	4 659.5	281.9	266.4	535.5	508.7	205.3	195.4
15–64	36 789.6	18 396.3	18 393.3	16 390.3	16 322.7	907.2	911.7	1 672.5	1 704.7	492.9	496.4
65 and over	8 417.0	3 299.9	5 116.8	2 936.7	4 537.2	171.9	268.1	277.0	452.0	74.3	114.2
0–4	3 582.0	1 836.8	1 745.2	1 605.6	1 527.0	91.3	86.6	168.4	159.6	68.8	66.0
5–9	3 364.3	1 728.2	1 636.1	1 498.4	1 417.3	86.0	80.8	161.3	153.1	64.7	61.8
10–14	4 223.9	2 168.9	2 055.1	1 813.2	1 715.2	104.6	99.0	205.8	196.0	71.8	67.6
15–19	4 729.1	2 430.4	2 298.6	2 077.1	1 973.2	116.5	112.6	231.2	220.8	76.3	70.6
20–24	4 499.3	2 275.7	2 223.6	2 059.6	2 005.2	114.2	113.7	220.1	211.0	71.3	65.5
25–29	3 893.0	1 962.8	1 930.2	1 763.8	1 727.9	91.2	88.8	186.6	182.3	56.1	56.3
30–34	3 847.5	1 934.7	1 912.8	1 690.8	1 667.0	91.0	89.9	173.3	171.2	49.9	49.1
35–39	4 023.4	2 018.7	2 004.7	1 829.5	1 817.2	98.2	98.6	171.6	171.0	49.2	49.6
40–44	3 246.7	1 632.5	1 614.4	1 487.5	1 461.8	83.5	81.8	145.1	149.5	44.0	44.8
45–49	3 118.2	1 564.0	1 554.2	1 400.5	1 384.6	77.8	76.8	141.2	147.8	39.1	40.8
50–54	3 115.3	1 544.3	1 570.9	1 350.8	1 358.2	76.0	77.0	139.7	150.5	36.7	39.7
55–59	3 142.2	1 535.4	1 606.8	1 347.4	1 396.8	78.2	81.6	136.5	149.8	35.7	39.7
60–64	3 174.9	1 497.8	1 677.1	1 383.3	1 530.8	80.6	90.9	127.2	150.8	34.6	40.3
65–69	2 567.7	1 154.9	1 412.7	979.6	1 185.8	59.8	73.3	98.5	128.5	26.9	34.1
70–74	2 402.1	1 012.7	1 389.4	907.8	1 233.3	52.8	72.7	86.1	124.3	23.1	32.4
75–79	1 771.6	662.3	1 109.2	607.8	1 003.2	34.4	59.0	55.2	97.9	14.3	23.8
80–84	1 039.6	322.6	717.0	304.4	660.9	17.0	38.2	25.9	61.7	6.7	14.5
85 and over	636.0	147.4	488.5	137.1	454.0	7.9	24.9	11.3	39.5	3.3	9.4

Note: Figures may not add due to rounding.
[1] 1983 figures.

Figure 5.1 *Tabulated data*
Sources: *Office of Population Censuses and Surveys, General Register Office (Scotland), General Register Office (Northern Ireland)*
(Reproduced with the permission of the Controller of Her Majesty's Stationery Office)

1. To make each number more compact, it has been divided by one thousand and rounded to one decimal place.

2. Column headings are aligned to the left-hand edge of the column.

3. Horizontal lines have been ruled only to separate headings and totals.

4. Rows have been grouped, with space left between every three or five items, or to identify a single item when appropriate.

5. There are no ruled vertical lines.

6. The numbers are aligned under the decimal points.

7. Space has been left between the thousands and the hundreds.

Bar charts

Bar charts are frequently used to show trends and variations. This is their primary purpose, and they should therefore not be made too complex: the information must be available at a glance. No more than two items should be compared on a single bar chart; if three items are needed, then three bar charts, with identical scales, drawn on the same page, will give this information more clearly than one bar chart which tries to cover all three. Bar charts drawn for comparative purposes must always have the same scale, or they will give the user a false impression of the comparison.

In a bar chart, information which is continuous should be represented by adjoining bars, for example, a chart showing annual rainfall, subdivided into monthly amounts, should be drawn with connecting bars. Obviously, August's rainfall starts where July's rainfall stops. On the other hand, discrete information should be shown by bars separated by space, for example, population figures counted once every five years should be shown by bars separated to show the missing years. Obviously, the population will not remain constant from the beginning of 1980 to the end of 1984.

Bars may be drawn either vertically or horizontally, preferably in such a way that the diagram has an overall landscape shape, as this is more pleasing to the eye.

The example shown in Figure 5.2 has been chosen as an illustration of how a bar chart can be used effectively. Its good qualities are listed below the figure on the next page.

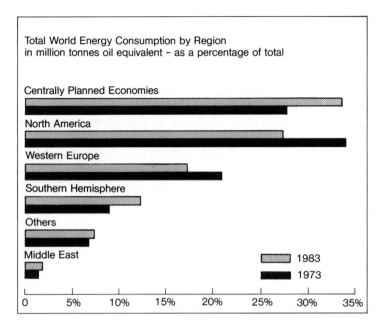

Figure 5.2 *Bar chart*

Source: Barclay's Review, May 1985. (Reproduced by kind permission of British Petroleum Company plc)

1. It shows only two items, 1973 and 1983.

2. The accurate figures are shown on the scale.

3. The bars give discrete information, and therefore each pair is separated from the others.

4. The diagram is clearly labelled.

5. The overall shape of the bar chart is landscape.

Pie charts

Pie charts are circular diagrams or 'pies' divided into slices, each representing a sub-division of the original amount. They emphasize divisions and proportions to the reader, who receives, however, an impression rather than a detailed picture. A pie should not be too complicated, and it is better to have two pie charts than one which has more divisions than the eye can cope with. Five slices is usually a sensible maximum. The difference in size between slices must be obvious to the user, and slices which are too close in size will be seen as identical: differences of less than 7° at the centre of segments will not be apparent to the report reader. It is helpful if small slices are placed horizontally, so that their labels can be written in a horizontal line.

A different form of diagram closely related to the pie chart is the percentage bar chart, in which a bar representing 100 per cent is used in place of a circle. It is divided into sections rather than slices, and although it is easier to draw than a pie chart, it makes less impact.

Graphs

If table are the most common form of diagram in a report, graphs are probably in second place. They have two distinct uses: they can give accurate scientific or similar results, and they can be used to show trends. If the data given are precise, it can be useful to give a table showing the points plotted on the graph, indeed, it may be important to do so. In principle, two versions of the same diagram are not recommended, and certainly it does not follow that if one version is unclear, the other will remove the confusion. Nevertheless, the presentation of scientific detail in both graphical and tabular forms can be an important exception to the general principle, and an aid to understanding.

The example given in Figure 5.3 (see page 75) has been chosen as an illustration of how a graph can be effectively presented. Its good qualities are listed below.

1. The scientific results shown on this graph will be discussed fully in the text, and are not therefore duplicated on the diagram itself. Essential notes have been kept to a minimum: it is, however, reasonable to explain A and B.

2. The lines A and B are labelled at the end of each curve.

3. Apart from the essential plotted points and lines, and the letters A and B, no material is added within the diagram. The illustrator has resisted the obvious temptation to write notes in the space at the lower right-hand corner of the graph.

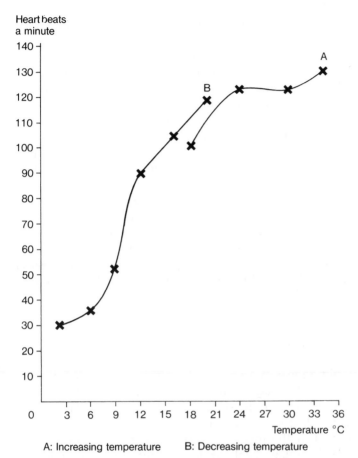

Figure 7.2 Effect of increasing and decreasing temperatures on the rate of heartbeat in tadpoles

Figure 5.3 *Graph*

4. The background grid has been omitted (although some of it could be drawn in if it were required).

5. The scales are clearly marked in a horizontal position.

6. The figure number and title are printed below the diagram, in such a position that confusion with the vertical scale is impossible.

7. A good margin on all sides of the figure enhances its appearance and prevents 'disappearance' into the binding.

While graphs are a useful and informative way of presenting data, they can be used, deliberately or otherwise, to mislead. A scale can be chosen which distorts the results (for instance, a vertical scale which does not begin at zero) so that the graph represents only a small part of the overall picture, and the trend shown is exaggerated. Occasionally, the vertical scale is omitted altogether, so that the graph line can be as steep or as level as its creator chooses. Two graphs which present similar information but which use different scales will appear to be a comparison of data, but will in fact mislead. In a report, it is essential that the user receives accurate information, and all such 'tricks' should be avoided.

The four most widely used forms of diagram have been discussed in this chapter, but even when the most appropriate forms have been chosen, and clearly and accurately produced, the problem of data presentation is not finished. There are still decisions to be made about the positioning of diagrams, their headings and notation, and checks to be made of their clarity to the user: they are usually clear enough to the person who has drawn them.

Positioning of diagrams

Diagrams should appear in a report where they are needed, that is, the convenience of the reader should again be paramount. If, as the reader works on the report, the situation is clarified by looking at the diagram, then the diagram should be in the text at the point at which it is to be studied. If the text says 'turn to page 21', or even 'turn overleaf', the reader will probably continue to read the prose unless or until it becomes essential to look at the diagram, by which time confusion may have already set in, as will irritation at having to search for the diagram. Sometimes the opposite problem occurs, and a diagram gets in the way of the reader because it breaks up the text. Long tables showing experimental or other results, for example, may be better placed at the end of the report in an appendix than in the text, where the reader would forget the prose as attention is deflected by rows of figures. Prose should never be broken abruptly, especially in mid-sentence, by a diagram.

Ideally, the diagram should be introduced, presented and discussed. If the diagram is referred to several times in the same report, then the writer has to decide whether to place it at the end, for overall convenience, or possibly to add it to a fold-out sheet which can be seen from any stage of the document. Diagrams which are not essential to the main readership of the report, but which are helpful to a minority, should appear in an appendix. Wherever diagrams are finally placed, the text must make their position absolutely clear, and no diagram or illustration should appear anywhere in a report if it is not referred to in the text.

Titles and numbers

Any diagram which does appear in the text must be clearly titled and numbered. As with report titles and headings (see Chapter 3), diagram titles should be as brief as possible, clearly stating what the diagram is about, without giving a full description. Titles should also clearly be titles, not placed in such a position that they appear to be labels on the illustration. The worst offence is to use up a space which occurs at the side of the diagram, when it can be unclear which diagram the title belongs to. The best position is underneath the diagram, and the most important rule is to be consistent in the positioning of titles throughout a report or series of reports.

Diagrams must have numbers as well as titles, for easy positioning and identification. The simplest, and therefore the best, method is to call all diagrams, whatever their form, Figures, and to give them two numbers separated by a decimal point. The first number will be the number of the major section in which the illustration occurs (as all diagrams in this chapter are identified by the first number, 5), and the second is the sequential number. So, Figure 5.7 is the seventh illustration in the fifth section of the report. It does not matter that Figure 5.7 appears in sub-section 5.2, or even sub-section 5.3.6: only the major section number is used. If the diagram appears in an appendix, then the identifying letter of that appendix precedes the numbers. So, Figure B3.2 is the second illustration in section 3 of Appendix B. The figure number should always precede the title of the figure, and be on the same line.

House styles about diagram labelling and positioning may have to take precedence over many of the recommendations made above. The practice of placing all diagrammatic material at the end of the report, irrespective of the reader's convenience, may initially save money, but it is to be deplored and, whenever possible, resisted. Sometimes the house style requires tables to be numbered separately from other figures (or even graphs and tables to be separate from each other and from the rest of the diagrams), but this can lead to confusion, for example between Table 3.2 and Figure 3.2, and it is not recommended. Whatever makes the diagrams easy to locate and easy to use is always worthwhile in terms of reader goodwill.

Photocopying

Copies of reports are usually produced by photocopying. If the original is clearly printed, then all the copies will be clear and easy to read. However, if there is a slight loss of clarity in the photocopying, and a letter becomes blurred or faint, the reader has to rely on the context in order to recognize the missing letter. Normally this causes little difficulty, and the reader will often read the word without even realizing that one letter is not clear. (This is not, of course, recommended, and the enormous problem of checking will be discussed in more detail in Chapter 6). The more serious problem arises when a number is unclear. The context will probably offer no clue as to what it should be, and if it is misread, the results might be very serious indeed, in either technical or financial terms. Some figures are particularly prone to confusion: 6, 8, and 5 quickly become indistinguishable, for example. If a number is sufficiently important to be included in a report, it must be read accurately. As writers, we are not the best judges of the clarity of either words or numbers: as we wrote them in the first place, we know what they should be, and will tend to read what we know, rather than what we see. It is wise to ask a colleague to read the numbers aloud while their author follows them on the page.

Space and shape

A page of typed or printed prose is usually neatly presented, with space at the top and bottom of the page and sensible margins to left and right. The writing is framed by space (although in passing, it is worth noting that the right-hand justification of type is less favoured than it used to be, with the general feeling that a 'ragged' edge is easier to read). This spacing of the page looks pleasant, it also allows room for the page number and a running title if there is one, and it prevents words being lost in the binding of the report. For some reason, this frame is often ignored if the page contains only diagrammatic material. The frame is just as important, as the page number must still be clear, and the diagram number and title should appear as a distinct entity with space underneath it. When numbers on diagrams collide with page numbers, confusion and, what is worse, errors can occur. In the same way, diagrams which disappear into the binding look untidy, and potentially important material is hidden. Lines on a graph should end at their frame, and not overflow onto the desk.

Space is also helpful within the diagram, assisting the eye to take in the information presented. The report writer should never be tempted to fill an empty area of a graph with words, or to add too much detail so that the reader is confused. The advantage of vertical and horizontal space in tables has already been discussed (see page 70). However, misuse of space is also confusing. If too much space is left between related items, the eye may lose track across the page, as happens sometimes on the contents page of a book, where the chapter headings are at the extreme left hand edge and the page numbers are far to the right. Indeed, if a larger space is left between related items than between unrelated items, the reader will search for the non-existent connection between the unrelated items.

We accept readily what is pleasing to the eye, often without realizing why we are doing so. It has been discovered that when a picture is presented in a landscape format it is more acceptable to the viewer than when it is presented in a portrait format (see Figure 5.4 on page 80). Therefore, the overall shape of a diagram should whenever possible be landscape. Often this can be achieved without turning the document, that is, when the diagram occupies less than a full page. If the document has to be turned, the turn must be in a clockwise direction, so that on a right-hand page a turned diagram will have its top towards the binding, while on the left-hand page the bottom will be towards the binding.

All information in a report should be clear to the intended reader. Diagrams are usually clear to their creator, who has after all spent considerable time and effort in producing them. They may be totally obscure or, perhaps more dangerously, ambiguous to the reader. The best way to check that the diagrams are clear is to beg or bribe a colleague to extract the information. If this is accurately done, then the reader can probably manage too.

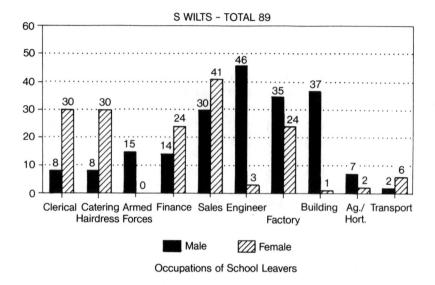

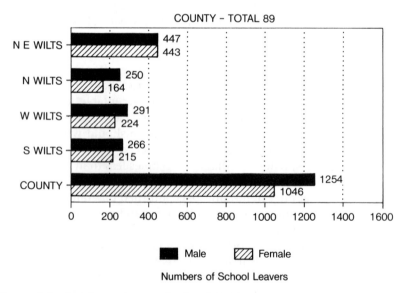

Figure 5.4   *Landscape formats for bar charts*

Source: School Leaver Destinations Digest 1989 and Trends 1986–1989. (Reproduced by kind permission of Wiltshire Guidance Services.)

Conclusion

The principles outlined in this chapter for achieving clarity in diagrams apply to other illustrations as well as those discussed. If a diagram is worth including in a report, even in the appendix, then it must be clear and usable. Blurred copies of photographs, regulations or computer print-outs are sometimes included in reports, or pages of advertising literature are poorly copied and added as appendices. If the material will not copy successfully, it must be produced in some other way, or omitted. Regulations, or complete print-outs with very small print or produced on a dot matrix printer, should be reprinted. Photographs must be clear, and black and white: if they cannot be copied successfully, they should be left out. Diagrams must always look good, supporting the text and adding to the overall impact of the document.

Some companies have arrangements for printing illustrations, and advice will be given about the preparation of copy. Even if such facilities exist, they are very expensive, and the writer of a small, in-company report might have to resort to do-it-yourself. For all producers of diagrammatic material, there is one final warning. You are responsible for abiding by the laws of copyright, and any illustration taken from a published document may be reproduced only with permission from the copyright holder.

Key points in Chapter 5

- Remember that diagrams should support the information in the text, presenting data in a format which is easy to assimilate.

- Follow a convention with which the reader is familiar.

- Give an appropriate amount of detail for the needs of the reader.

- Ensure that your tables allow the reader to scan vertically and to find related information horizontally.

- You can use graphs to show detailed scientific data or general trends; remember that empty spaces within a graph are important to the understanding of the data.

- Your diagrams should be easily accessible to the reader, but don't let them interrupt the flow of information.

- Make sure that all your diagrams have a number and a short title.

- Check that your diagrams are both accurate and pleasing to the eye.

CHAPTER 6

Revision and checking

*Meeting the objectives · Clarification of headings · Checklist for revision ·
In-company considerations · Confidentiality · Checking the text ·
Consistency · Copies of the text · Report storage · Binding*

In the middle of writing words and preparing diagrams, you might think that the producer of reports was fully occupied, and that revision was something that happened later, if there was time. This is a mistake. Revision of a report starts when the format (Chapter 3) is chosen and the material is organized, stages which, as we have seen, precede the writing. The writing itself may not begin at the beginning, which is another good reason for constant revision until the last available moment.

Meeting the objectives

The report writer will have identified the readership and clarified the terms of reference. The objective of the report will have been written out in a sentence or a short paragraph. People being people, the writer may well forget all of this, being carried away by the most original, impressive, interesting or simply time-consuming aspects of the work. Revision is, then, the checking back, the regular reference to all those initial decisions in order to make sure that the report is still going in the right direction. It is easy to be side-tracked. A group of students, asked to write a report 'selling' their home town as a site for relocation to a 'company' which was considering Edinburgh as an alternative, found that they knew a good deal about the facilities offered by the town they worked in, but they had to put time and effort into finding out about the counter-attractions of Edinburgh. Unfortunately, they were so carried away by their own initiative and information-seeking that they ended up by producing reports which 'sold' Edinburgh. It was as well for their future employment that the reports were part of an exercise and not part of 'real life'!

The danger is a real one, however. Reports which cover a limited geographical area may wander outside their limits; reports may stress the problems at the expense of the recommendations, they may recommend what is technically appropriate while overlooking the personnel implications. The balance of the report has to be revised to make sure that it is the balance originally intended, and that the writer's enthusiasm (or indeed distaste) has not prejudiced the outcome.

Clarification of headings

It is also necessary to revise the headings. As was suggested in Chapter 3, the original general headings usually have to be made more specific, to ensure that they are as helpful as possible to the report user. They may also need to be re-arranged, to make their logical progression helpful and clear; the information within a section may need to be moved around to produce a more efficient result, and even the words in a sentence may be changed in order to produce the correct emphasis.

Checklist for revision

If the report production takes a week, the writer may sensibly spend half an hour each day revising what has been prepared and asking if there is any better way to present the information than that which has been chosen. A good way of answering the question might be to take a 'purple passage', the section of which the writer is most proud, and to subject it to the following analysis:

Is this relevant to what I am trying to do?
Is this relevant to what the reader/user will want?
Does this passage fit into the pattern of the whole report?
Is the organization clear, logical and easy to use?

Is the material divided into manageable chunks (sections, sub-sections or paragraphs)?
Does each sentence add to the meaning—and is it grammatically correct?
Does each word add to the meaning—and is it used precisely?
Will the reader/user *also* consider this to be a highlight of the report?

If the honest answer to any of these questions is 'no', then revision is clearly called for. It will in the long run save time (that of the authorizing authority and the client) and will bring about a faster response.

In-company considerations

Revision by the report writer is a good thing; revision by the writer's superior may be questioned. It is often helpful, especially if the supervisor (branch head, head of department or whoever) discusses with the writer the changes which are required, or at least adds positive comments to the work which has been produced. It is not at all helpful if changes are made to the writer's style, not because it is bad, but because it is different from that of the superior. Writing style is an individual matter and, while house style should be adhered to, changes to an acceptable personal style can be hurtful. They may also be counter-productive, as they are often obvious to the reader, who may be disturbed in the reading by a sudden and inexplicable change of reading pattern. While it is often useful to have technical and legal content checked by a higher authority, and any ambiguity or illogicality questioned, change for the sake of change (the 'I must make my mark' syndrome) is bad for morale. Young employees whose reports have been changed beyond recognition—and nobody has told them why—may well resent their superiors' attitudes and lose confidence in their own work. Of course 'political' considerations will weigh heavily on more senior staff, but a few words of explanation (or indeed an explanation that an explanation is impossible for reasons of confidentiality) will help junior staff to accept what at first sight seems to be meaningless interference.

Confidentiality

Confidentiality is an important consideration in the production of reports, for various reasons. The information contained in the report may be highly sensitive, possibly affecting national security. It may include research data which are confidential to the company whose scientists produced the report, or financial details which could be useful to a rival company. Reports often have commercial implications, and are at least temporarily confidential to a small number of people. In such cases, it is essential to record the number of existing copies of a particular report, with each copy stating clearly which number it is, and of what total. Library records may not show that the report exists (although clearly some record must be kept of the whereabouts of all copies), or may indicate the existence of the report but show also that it is not available for general use.

However, confidentiality extends beyond the company responsible for the report: it may include information provided by outside bodies which do not wish to be identified. The normal acknowledgement of outside help must then be omitted, but the revision of the report should include a careful check that confidentiality has not been breached by accident. Reference to a particular product might identify a research establishment; a photograph of a notable building will identify architect, construction company and possibly a wide range of sub-contractors to other people in the same industry. If a report writer has the slightest hesitation about including confidential material, there is a moral obligation to check with the source, just as the 'real-life' examples used in this book are given only with permission from the original companies. There is, naturally, also an obligation to treat the resulting information as a confidential document while the report writing is in progress: it is not unknown for report writers and readers to feel 'safe' on a commuter train, regardless of the unusually close proximity of unknown fellow-travellers!

Checking the text

In an ideal world, each important report would be checked by two people, neither of them the author. One would check for technical accuracy and conformity to company policy; the other would read the text for clarity of expression, grammatical accuracy and obvious keyboarding errors which had been missed by the computer's spell-check (see Chapter 4). Both would have plenty of time in which to carry out these duties, which would be recognized as important stages in the production of a report.

Even in a world far from ideal, it is still worth while to have the most prestigious (or expensive) reports checked in this way. Inaccurate information will undermine confidence in a company's technical expertise. Perhaps surprisingly, so will printing errors. The reader may reasonably feel that an organization of high reputation and advanced technology will know its facts, and that the error which produces 'modern' for 'modem' will be recognized for what it is, a slip of the word processor. However, the reader may feel less reasonable on finding details of costings given with the heading, 'The prices listde below ...'. Both these examples are real-life, as is that of the report writer who transformed 'There is *not* a substantial amount of water in the brickwork' into 'There is *now* a substantial amount of water in the brickwork'. No computer spellcheck (see Chapter 4) would pick up such a mistake, but as the intended meaning is reversed, the effect could be highly damaging to a company's professional reputation.

The technical content of a report is usually checked by the writer's superior or a well-disposed colleague; the frequently forgotten aspect is the printing. Word processors tend, against popular opinion, to increase the number of errors; just because it is so easy to change a word or sentence, the author may check less thoroughly. It seems a pity to interrupt the flow of inspiration just because a wrong key has been pressed—and so the writer carries on, with good intentions about making corrections later.

The report's author is in any case the most inefficient person at checking for errors. We all tend to see what we know we have written, whether or not it is in front of us on the screen or the page (a thorough check should always be made from a print-out; the screen is at a bad angle for checking, and reveals too limited an amount of text at a time). A friend or colleague will check without preconceptions about what has been written and so is much more likely to notice mistakes.

In spite of this, report writers often have to check their own work, and do so under unrealistic time constraints. If the writing can be left alone for 48 hours, the checking will be more thorough than it would be if carried out sooner. This is the time-lag which seems to allow a writer to forget the exact words used and therefore to look at what is on the page rather than to try to remember it. The accuracy of checking increases with the time-lag, and a report left for a week can be checked reasonably well by its author. Realistically, a week is rarely available, and even 48 hours appears often to be a luxury.

There are, however, some guidelines for checking one's own work. Perhaps the most important is that concentration during checking does not last long; half an hour spent on checking is reasonable while two hours is not. Even a short break after the half-hour will improve concentration when work is resumed. Within the half-hour, it is helpful both to concentration and to the avoidance of eye-strain if the focal length of viewing is changed. Simply refocusing the eyes for a moment on the most distant object available, before returning to the checking process, is useful.

Most writers are fascinated by their own work, and it is easy to be distracted by the brilliance of the sentence further down the page and so to forget the error-filled lines which come first. Covering all of the page below the line which is being checked, and revealing the text one line at a time, slows down the reading usefully, and ensures concentration on each line in turn. A ruler is too narrow for this, but a blank sheet of paper moved slowly down the page is a satisfactory alternative. Numbers may be checked one at a time, left to right, in the same way. Sets of figures (financial or statistical data, for example) are better checked by two people working together, one reading the figures while the other checks the page. This device should not, however, be used for the written text, as one or other of the two will usually lose concentration without the fact being obvious to the partner. 'Please would you go through the last paragraph again as I didn't notice what you said' is not a request likely to make future working relationships cordial.

It has been assumed so far that checking consists of looking for a wrong word. Much more is involved, not least the need to check the *whole* text, title page, appendices, diagrams included. The title page is often taken for granted, and the mis-spelling of the author's name, or the name of his company, is not unknown.

Some errors do not involve a different word, or even a mis-spelt word. The same word repeated at the same point of a line, on consecutive lines, looks odd on the page. Usually a rearrangement of the sentence (or Roget's *Thesaurus*), will solve the problem. Words or letters can be accidentally repeated, especially at a page turnover, or divided at an awkward point (the most notorious example of this is probably the incorrect division of 'therapist'). The importance of such oddities on the page is not primarily loss of meaning, but loss of confidence. The reader, however favourably inclined to the material of the report, begins to doubt the information if its appearance suggests a careless approach.

Consistency

The same problem of reader goodwill makes consistency important. It does not matter whether U.S.A. appears in this form or as USA, but it matters to the reader if the usage is inconsistent. In the case of a published report, the copy-editor will tidy up such details, but for the vast number of typed reports, it has to be the job of the writer. When alternative forms of a word or abbreviation are possible, the report must be consistent in order to impress. Editorial decisions may be part of company policy, but when options exist, the writer must make a choice and then stick to it.

Copies of the text

So, finally, the report is completed, revised and thoroughly checked. The next stage will often be photocopying. Even this stage can go wrong. A report with clearly numbered pages (full marks!) ran into trouble when it was found that the copies had pages numbered 1 to 6, 7, 7, and 9 onwards. The photocopier (human or machine) had obviously dozed off. Pages can be moved, so that they appear with the text sloping, or partly missing, or blank ... the possibilities are endless. It seems churlish, after so much careful checking, to ask that the pages are collated by hand, but a random sample check might reveal a problem which affects a number of copies.

Report storage

In preparing a report, the writer must be aware of the need to keep a back-up copy of all the work to date; it may also be necessary to keep a copy of the original report if it is subsequently updated or modified. In most systems, editing will over-write the original.

Reports which are stored on the company's system need an

appropriate file reference for ease of identification (see Chapter 3). Indeed, if the report is to be stored for an indefinite period, the system on which it was created must remain available; the threat of computer 'viruses' is restricting the mobility of information stored on disc from one system to another.

Binding

Reports are still circulated for the most part as printed documents. Some are stapled, some put into ring binders, or spiral binding, or various forms of book binding, according to their length, their importance and their distribution. The writer often has little say in this stage, but is entitled to complain if there are too many pages for the binding, so that it splits, or if the binding chosen will not stand up to the heavy use to which the report is put. Reports used under heavy industrial conditions might need to be prepared on grease-resistant paper, with covers that can be wiped clean, but such requirements are not common. What the writer of reports should ask for is that the report, the result of so much hard work, will look good enough to create the reader response hoped for since the project began.

Key points in Chapter 6

- Check that the report continues to fulfil its objectives, and that the author's prejudices have not affected the presentation of the evidence.

- Submit your 'purple passages' to vigorous checking, for relevance and for appropriate presentation.

- Reports are often commercially or technically sensitive; make sure that you keep such information confidential.

- Poor checking results in wrong information and a loss of confidence on the part of the reader. Check your report carefully— and ask a colleague to check it, too.

- Remember that consistency is important, as is accurate copying.

- Ensure that the binding of your report is appropriate to the use to which it will be put, and to its status.

CHAPTER 7

Specimen management report

This chapter consists of the making of a management report, from the initial problem to the final document as it will be distributed. As far as possible we have followed, stage by stage, the problems which might confront the report writer, and have shown how these problems can be tackled. Although the order of events is thus chronological, we have also indicated the way in which the preliminary organization will be modified as the work proceeds. The company, its problems and its reports are entirely fictitious.

Background

The Head Office of JAE Foods Ltd is in a large office block on an industrial estate on the outskirts of Basingstoke. About 300 personnel work at Head Office, and facilities appear to be good: a subsidized canteen for all staff, a licensed dining room for senior managers and visitors, and vending machines on each floor, dispensing hot and cold drinks. About a year ago, flexitime working was introduced; this was welcomed and is operating successfully.

Problem

Recently, the Catering Officer has reported a change in usage of the canteen. The number of meals served is falling, and so is the income. The Canteen Manager, who reports directly to the Catering Officer, agrees that while he has maintained a high standard of food, the financial position of the canteen is beginning to cause alarm. These comments have been brought to the attention of the Managing Director, who asks the Catering Officer to supply her with a report on the staffing and cost of both canteen and dining room. At the same time, she asks one of the Personnel staff, assisted by the Personnel Manager's secretary, to produce a second report which investigates possible changes in staff eating habits, with conclusions and/or recommendations as appropriate. (It is the latter report which is the subject of this chapter. Personnel agreement and union support have, it is assumed, been obtained.)

This is the problem as it is put to Jill Miles, Personnel Officer. She prepares her Terms of Reference and tries to write out the objective of the report very briefly, in order to clarify her own ideas and to introduce the report.

TERMS OF REFERENCE

As Personnel Officer for JAE Foods Ltd, I have been asked by Frances Leighton, Managing Director, to report on the reasons for the decline in canteen usage, considering the implications of current staff eating habits and recommending changes in catering provision which might prove helpful to the staff. A parallel report by Philip Jenkins, Catering Officer, will consider staffing and financial implications. Both reports will be available to Mrs Leighton by the end of February, 1991.

OBJECTIVE

Why are fewer people eating in the canteen, and where are they eating instead? Can we get them back?

Jill has clearly discussed her report with her senior managers in order to clarify exactly what she is to investigate. She has picked up the comment that 'we must try to provide what's best for the staff, to keep up morale apart from anything else', and she has checked on the time available to her (about three weeks). The Terms of Reference will appear in the final report; the Objective is Jill's own—hence the informal language.

Procedure

Having made sure that she understands her brief, Jill decides on the procedure which she and Mary, the Personnel Manager's secretary, will have to follow in order to obtain the information on which to base the report. They decide that it would be useful to produce a questionnaire, which would be distributed to all staff. Bearing in mind the difficulty of persuading people to complete and return questionnaires, Jill decides to delegate one person in each open-plan office to ask the questions directly of each staff member, recording the answers on the prepared sheet. The process should not take more than three or four minutes in each case, and the questions must therefore be short and few in number. Mary agrees to organize the questionnaire distribution and to collate the replies. Jill and Mary then prepare the questionnaire; only the analysis of replies is important to the body of the report, but a copy of the questionnaire itself is of use to the reader, and it will therefore become: **APPENDIX A. QUESTIONNAIRE.**

While Mary works on the questionnaire distribution, Jill needs to find out the comparative figures for hot and cold canteen meals over the past year, and to check on canteen opening times. She will also look briefly at the figures for dining room usage, in case they have any bearing on the question, and will find out whether the vending machines are providing more or fewer cups of coffee, tea, etc., than in the past. Personal observation is also important: Jill will talk to the Canteen Manager, and ask a random selection of employees for their comments; she and Mary will use the canteen at different times each day for a week.

The information generated by all this procedure will be the main body of the report. However, Jill decides that the procedure itself deserves to be recorded, as it will identify for the reader the basis of the findings. (Note that if Jill or Mary had consulted documents, previous reports, or articles, for instance, they would at this stage have started to compile a set of references or a bibliography.)

---

2 PROCEDURE

(1) A short questionnaire (see Appendix A) was presented to all available members of staff, and their replies were recorded.

(2) Interviews were held informally with:
Canteen Manager (Miss S Hyde)
Catering Officer (Mr P Jenkins)
15 members of staff (5% of the total, selected at random)

(3) Mary Pringle and I used the canteen each working day for a week, and recorded our own observations.

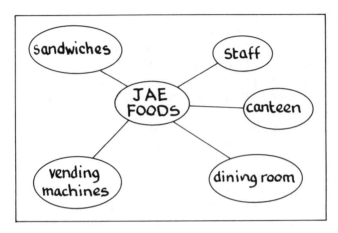

Figure 7.1   *Spider base*

As Jill and Mary proceed with their enquiries, they discover a new factor. A snacks and sandwich bar has opened a few hundred yards from JAE Foods Ltd Head Office, and the owners have started delivering sandwiches at prearranged times to a number of office blocks in the area. This service is proving highly popular, and groups of staff in several offices now combine to telephone an order for sausage rolls and sandwiches, which are delivered at specified times during the day. Deliveries are available from 11 a.m. to 4 p.m., provided that the order is received by 10 a.m. As the canteen has an area reserved for personnel who bring their own food, Mary takes particular note of its usage: it is often crowded. There is, incidentally, no rule against staff eating or drinking at their desks, except where there are computers.

Jill can already see a pattern to her investigation, and she draws the base (Figure 7.1) for the spider diagram on which she will gather all her information.

As the reactions from interviews and questionnaires arrive, the information will be added to the appropriate 'bubble'. Staff reaction will be a constant factor, but the other 'bubbles' on the spider base will probably produce headings from which Jill can form her contents list. For the moment, she finds her material in a random way, but the following information is of note.

1.   The canteen, which is self-service, is open from 12.30 to 2.15.

2. The dining room is available for evening functions. Its use, day and evening, has not changed significantly during the past year.

3. The canteen is serving fewer hot meals than in previous years; the trend seems to be steadily downwards.

4. The vending machines are heavily used: tea, coffee and squash sales are all substantially up on previous years.

5. Queues in the canteen are small, except at 12.30 when the canteen opens.

The questionnaire produced 180 replies. Staff reported that the canteen food was of good quality and reasonable in price, but there were many complaints from staff who chose to start work early, that they were hungry before 12.30. Eight staff requested that the canteen be open in the late afternoon for high tea. Many staff said that they preferred to order sandwiches, as this enabled them to save time over lunch and, because of flexitime, to finish early or 'save up' time off for an extra half-day. The vending machines were popular, but there were complaints that they were sometimes empty and that at mid-morning and mid-afternoon there were queues for the machines.

In the face of all this information, and a great deal of related detail, Jill decides that much more organization is needed before she can start to write her report. She goes back to her spider base, and adds each piece of information, noting it as a key word or phrase only (the original information can be looked up during the actual writing). First, she deals with Mary's analysis of the questionnaire replies, adding information to appropriate 'bubbles'; then she adds the results of interviews, and lastly her own and Mary's observations. The spider is now complete (see Figure 7.2 on page 97).

The advantage to Jill of using the spider is that each piece of information in turn can be added to the appropriate place (and subsequently moved if necessary). Had she listed points under the same headings, she would have had to scan the questionnaire responses for information concerning the canteen, then scan the manager's comments for information about the canteen, and then look for related information in her own and Mary's notes. The whole process of scanning would then be repeated for the vending machines, and then for the dining room, and then for the sandwich bar: a very cumbersome and time-consuming process. From the spider format, it is comparatively easy to draw conclusions and to see connections; for example, the link between flexitime and the desire for earlier canteen opening.

The contents list which began with the spider base diagram can now be drawn up in detail, and Jill does this:

CONTENTS

1   **INTRODUCTION**

2   **PROCEDURE**

3   **CANTEEN**
3.1   Staff responses
3.2   Interview with Canteen Manager
3.3   Observations

4   **DINING ROOM**
4.1   Staff responses
4.2   Interview with Catering Officer
4.3   Observations

5   **VENDING MACHINES**
5.1   Staff responses
5.2   Interview with Catering Officer
5.3   Observations

6   **SANDWICH BAR**
6.1   Staff responses
6.2   Observations

7   **CONCLUSIONS**

8   **RECOMMENDATIONS**

APPENDIX A. QUESTIONNAIRE

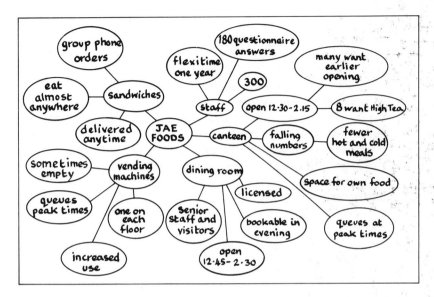

Figure 7.2 *Completed spider*

Sections 7 and 8 might need sub-division, but it is difficult to be sure at this stage. Jill can, however, now start writing her report, and she will most probably start with section 3, 4, 5 or 6: it does not matter which. The language she uses is, of course, formal, but since the report will be seen only by the staff of JAE Foods Ltd, she is allowed to use the first person ('I observed that ... '), and she does so. One section of the main body of the report reads as follows:

---

3 CANTEEN

The self-service canteen is open on Monday to Friday from 12.30 to 2.15. There is seating for 95 people, including some tables reserved for staff who bring their own food.

3.1 Staff responses

It was generally agreed that the quality of the food was good and the subsidized price reasonable.

The question of hours of opening produced the following comments:

(1) Staff who begin work at 8.00 would like the canteen to be open for lunch before 12.30.

> (2) Eight members of staff who frequently work in the evening would like the canteen to serve high tea in the late afternoon.
>
> (3) Many staff complained that queues at 12.30 meant a long wait (up to 10 minutes) before they could be served their food. An earlier start, it was suggested, would ease the queue problem.
>
> **3.2 Interview with Canteen Manager**
>
> The Canteen Manager reported that the number of hot and cold meals served had decreased steadily over the previous eight months.
>
> Nevertheless, she was aware that queues formed just before 12.30, and that those who arrived at exactly 12.30 sometimes had to wait up to 10 minutes before reaching the self-service area.
>
> **3.3 Observations**
>
> Visits by the report writers to the canteen suggested that queues were rare, except at 12.30, when they seemed to build up quickly.
>
> The canteen area reserved for staff who brought their own food was full on several occasions during the week of observation (16–20 February 1991).

On the basis of this evidence and that of the rest of the report, Jill can come to specific conclusions. She will not at this point suggest what action should be taken, nor will she introduce any new evidence. Part of the conclusions section is given below.

> **7 CONCLUSIONS**
>
> (1) The canteen is used less than in the past, apart from the area reserved for those who bring their own food.
>
> (2) Staff are dissatisfied with the present opening hours of the canteen, especially since the introduction of flexitime.
>
> (3) Many staff order sandwiches, to be delivered at any convenient time during the day, from the sandwich bar.
>
> (4) Use of the vending machines has increased rapidly during the past year.
>
> (5) Use of the dining room has shown no significant change.

It is helpful to list the conclusions in this way, as many readers will find this section and the recommendations particularly useful. In this case, the Managing Director may read only these parts of the report. Jill can be subjective in her recommendations, provided that all she recommends is firmly based on the evidence presented. This will be the next section of the report to be written.

---

8 RECOMMENDATIONS

In the light of the above conclusions, I recommend that consideration be given to extending the opening hours of the canteen at lunch time, preferably by allowing lunch to be served from 12.00 onwards.

There is insufficient demand to warrant opening the canteen at any time other than at lunchtime.

Vending machines are heavily used, and I recommend that more be provided, perhaps two on each floor instead of the present one.

The provision of sandwiches is obviously very popular, especially as they can be eaten at any time during the working day. I suggest that the possibility of our own canteen supplying sandwiches, perhaps for an hour before lunch, be investigated.

Sandwiches might be ordered on the previous day, and delivered to each department in the morning, if demand is sufficient. The current use of the sandwich bar suggests that this would be an additional service welcomed by the staff.

The report is now well on its way to completion. As it seems likely that copies will be circulated to all senior staff, Jill considers the need for a summary. The report is not long (perhaps five or six pages in all), but a summary will emphasize her conclusions and recommendations, and will be useful in reminding her readers of the subject of the report. On balance, she decides that it is worth writing a very short summary, as an *aide-mémoire* and for those who will never find time to read the whole report. Jill sets herself a limit of 100 words. Her first version covers the ideas adequately, but is too long (see top of page 100).

SUMMARY

This report <u>investigates</u> the recent decline in the use of the canteen,

and <u>considers</u> other means of food and drink provision ~~for staff~~ at

Head Office. Investigation shows that since the introduction of
                extended lunch time opening
flexitime, staff need ~~lunch earlier than allowed by the 12.30 opening~~.

~~Indeed,~~ many prefer to order sandwiches from a local ~~sandwich bar~~
                                          source

~~rather than eat in the canteen~~. They ~~then~~ buy ~~hot or cold~~ drinks from
                       therefore
the vending machines, which are over-used ~~as a result~~.
    I
~~The report therefore~~ recommends that lunchtime opening hours for
                   with
the canteen are extended, ~~and that~~ the possibility of the canteen itself
                                more
serving sandwiches. ~~should be investigated~~. ~~A greater number of~~
          urgently
vending machines are needed.

(114 words)

Jill now cuts out unnecessary words ('therefore' instead of 'as a result'), and omitted unnecessary detail (the opening time of the canteen, for instance). She tidies up her style ('investigates' and 'Investigation' at the beginning), and stresses the urgency of extra vending machines, as this can probably be implemented while the other suggestions are being discussed, a move which will raise staff morale. Her final version is well within her word limit:

SUMMARY

In this report, I have considered food and drink provision for Head Office personnel, and investigated the reasons for the decline in use of the canteen.

Since the introduction of flexitime, many staff find the canteen opening hours too restricted, prefer to order sandwiches from an outside source, and buy drinks from the over-used vending machines in the Head Office building.

Extended lunchtime opening hours for the canteen are recommended, with the possibility of the canteen itself serving sandwiches. Additional vending machines are urgently needed.

(85 words)

Jill now finishes the report, adding a simple title page.

JAE FOODS LTD
Maple Drive
Basingstoke, Hampshire

**THE PROVISION OF FOOD AND DRINK
FOR HEAD OFFICE STAFF**

JILL MILES
25 February, 1991

The contents list will follow the title page, then the summary, and then the full report with its pages numbered. As there are no references or bibliography, the report will conclude with Appendix A (the questionnaire). It is now Jill's responsibility to check the report for accuracy and presentation, and she has wisely left herself a couple of days in which to do this. Her name and the date are already on the title page, but she may feel that she should also sign the document personally, at the end of the text but before the appendix. As the report will have a small, internal circulation, the pages may simply be copied, stapled together, and put in a plain plastic cover.

Jill Miles is pleased with her report, but the final judgement will be that of her Managing Director. If the recommendations form a useful basis for further discussion, the report can be considered a success.

CHAPTER 8

Specimen technical report

In outline, this chapter is similar to Chapter 7, but the specimen report which it contains is based on engineering information. Again, we have followed, stage by stage, the procedure of organising and writing the report; in this case we have used a real-life situation as a basis, with details changed to preserve confidentiality.

Background

In the mid-1980s, it became clear that a new bridge was needed over the River Abb to carry a major road leading to a newly-opened stretch of motorway. An architect was commissioned, and in due course a fine-looking bridge was built and the traffic routed accordingly. The bridge was officially opened by a member of the Royal Family, and all seemed well.

Problem

However, it was not long before complaints started to reach local councillors, the police, and eventually the Environmental Health Officer in the nearby market town of Abiford. When the wind came from a particular direction, the bridge made a disturbing noise—a whining sound sufficiently loud to keep the local residents awake at night. As the wind direction happened to be the prevailing one, the problem occurred frequently and there were increasingly vociferous demands for action.

The County Surveyor's Office, when the problem was put to them, asked a couple of their bridge engineers to investigate. They discovered that the vibration of the bridge parapet could be felt simply by touching it; tests showed the frequency range of the problem, and that there were very lightly damped resonances of the structure within this frequency range.

This is the problem as it is presented to Andrew Poynter, a research acoustics engineer at the nearby university. His terms of reference are as follows:

TERMS OF REFERENCE

Following a large number of complaints from local residents about the noise made by the Abiford Bridge when the wind came from the south-west, Andrew Poynter, consultant engineer employed by Abimouth University, was asked by the County Council to investigate the cause of the noise and to suggest a remedy. The nature of the wind excitation was excluded from the investigation.

 The County Surveyor's Office asked that the proposed solution should not change the outward appearance of this architect-designed bridge.

Objectives

On receiving the request and accepting the terms offered, Andrew identifies his objectives as:

(1) to find the cause of the vibration and therefore of the noise;
(2) to suggest a remedy which would leave the appearance of the bridge unchanged.

Procedure

A 2m length section of the bridge parapet, constructed from hollow steel tubes, has been removed and sent to Abimouth for tests to determine the nature of the vibration and, therefore, the likely cause of the noise.

 Andrew Poynter wants to measure the vibration characteristics of the parapet in the range 100 Hz to 4000 Hz, and to examine possible

cures which would damp out any measured vibration in the range
1 kHz–2 kHz. He decides on two possible methods:

(1) filling the whole section with dry sand;
(2) attaching a damping medium to the uprights.

The tests are to be carried out in the Structures Laboratory at Abimouth
University. From these initial decisions, Andrew makes notes for the
Procedure section of his report. He can also plan the beginning of his
Contents List, following the usual format for laboratory test reports.

CONTENTS

SUMMARY

1   INTRODUCTION (containing TERMS OF REFERENCE)

2   PROCEDURE

3   TESTS ON THE PARAPET SECTION AS RECEIVED
3.1   Vibration tests over a range of frequencies
3.2   Results
3.3   Mode shape survey
3.4   Results

4   SAND INFILL TEST
4.1   Test procedure
4.2   Results

5   DAMPING STRIP TEST
5.1   Test procedure
5.2   Results

6   CONCLUSIONS

7   RECOMMENDATIONS

The first tests on the parapet section as it was received can now be
carried out. [N.B. *In 'real-life', further tests would be appropriate, but we*

have simplified the procedure for the purposes of this report.] Andrew makes notes of the equipment he is using, and on the process, and writes up Section 3 of the report as soon as he can. As it is written for an outside body, he is careful to use a formal style, and he includes a diagram to make the measurement and excitation positions clear to his readers. This section of the report reads as follows:

3.1 Vibration tests over a range of frequencies

The parapet section (see Figure 3.1) was mounted in the laboratory by suspending it from two 3mm steel cables attached at each end to the top handrail. A small vibration exciter was attached at point A in the sketch and excited the parapet in the indicated direction. The exciter was driven by a beat frequency oscillator which has an automatic sweep capacity, through a power amplifier.

An automatic control was set up to give a constant force amplitude throughout the frequency range. As the damping of the structure was known to be very light, the sweep rate had to be relatively slow: the sweep from 100 Hz to 4 kHz took 15 minutes to complete.

The vibration was measured using an accelerometer with a suitable charge amplifier, the position of the accelerometer being moved during the tests to three representative positions numbered 1, 2 and 3 in Figure 3.1. The output of the accelerometer was fed to a level recorder using frequency calibrated charts which were automatically advanced by means of a drive from the beat frequency oscillator.

Once these tests are completed, Andrew records his results, producing the appropriate diagrams on his computer and giving Figure 3.1 the title *Parapet test section.* As he is anxious to try out his first potential solution to the vibration problem—filling the parapet section with sand to observe the effect on the general vibration characteristics—he leaves his notes on the computer, to be written up formally when the tests are completed.

This sand infill test is now carried out and recorded; the relevant section begins like this:

---

4   SAND INFILL TEST
4.1 Test procedure

The procedure for this test was exactly the same as that described in 3.1, each of the three configurations previously used being tested again.

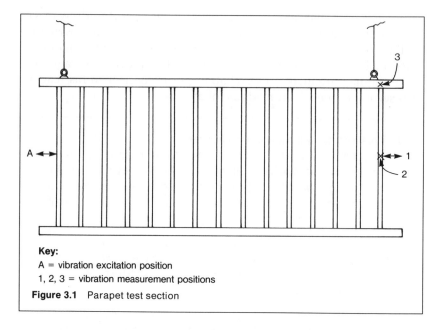

Key:
A = vibration excitation position
1, 2, 3 = vibration measurement positions
Figure 3.1   Parapet test section

The results are recorded as before, and Andrew proceeds to the damping strip test. He decides that he can carry out this test adequately by using one strip of aluminium alloy sheet with damping resin on one side, although he realises that this would be too expensive a material to use on the full bridge parapet. He writes up this test.

---

5   DAMPING STRIP TEST

5.1   Test procedure

As an alternative to the infill of sand as a vibration damping medium, a damping strip was used which consisted of a piece of 22 gauge aluminium alloy sheet with damping resin on one side. This strip was attached to the surface of one of the uprights on the opposite side to the accelerometer, using a blowlamp. Vibration testing was then carried out as described in 3.1.

Andrew's laboratory tests are now complete, and he can assemble the resulting data for assessment. Each test has its own results, and he is sure that he made the right decision in reporting the results after each procedure rather than all at the end. He can now write up each

Results section; that for the sand infill tests is given below. Note that he does not need to produce the report in the 'right' order—5.1 is completed before 4.2, simply because it is easier this way. Obviously, on the computer all the sections appear in order.

4.2 Results

This test was carried out in exactly the same way as that described in 3.1, but it is sufficient to show the comparison for one configuration only. The results are shown in Figure 4.1, and can be compared directly with those in Figure 3.2. It will be seen that the behaviour was very similar at low frequency, except that the three resonances were moved down the frequency scale as a result of the increased mass (due to the sand infill). There was no attenuation at this point.

However, in the critical 1 kHz–2 kHz band, the vibration activity was significantly reduced, and there appeared to be one resonance only at about 1250 Hz. This implied that the sand infill was successful in reducing vibration levels in the critical band.

Andrew has now completed the evidence on which his Conclusions and Recommendations sections are to be based. He is satisfied that the results he obtained for the natural frequencies of the parapet section agree broadly with those of the original tests on the bridge, and that the tests on the 2m section are therefore properly representative of the whole structure. This point is made at the beginning of the Conclusions section. Andrew also assesses the problems of applying either of his solutions, and discusses these; the Conclusions read in part as follows.

---

6 CONCLUSIONS

The results of the tests described above have shown that the vibration damping provided by using a fine dry sand infill in the parapet was effective in the critical frequency range, 1 kHz–2kHz. This solution appeared to be acceptable, although there could be considerable difficulty in getting the sand to penetrate all the cavities in the structure.

On the other hand, the vibration damping provided by the attachment of a damping strip to a single upright was not satisfactory, although if all the uprights were to be treated, the results might be improved. This would have the advantage of relative simplicity, but the strips themselves would not be vandal-proof.

Although Andrew feels that on balance the sand infill is the better solution, he would like on-site tests to be carried out before the Council makes its final decision. His recommendation makes this clear:

---

7   RECOMMENDATIONS

In the light of the laboratory tests described above, it is recommended that tests be carried out on the Abiford site in order to make a direct comparison between the effects of the wind on parapet sections with and without a sand infill.

All the material for the main body of the report is now drafted on Andrew's computer. He finalizes his text and checks a printout carefully. There is a series of diagrams to be added (Figure 3.1 is given above as an example), and because of their number, he decides to keep them all at the end of the report, with a Contents List of Figures at the beginning to help the reader.

There remains the Summary. Andrew is aware of the importance of a good summary, and allows himself plenty of time to prepare it. He takes some of the background material from the Introduction, includes only a brief reference to the tests themselves, and concentrates on his results and recommendation. As both are short, he reckons that he is unlikely to need more than 100 words for his summary, and so it proves.

SUMMARY

At the request of the County Council, a section of the parapet of Abiford Bridge was removed for the investigation at Abimouth University of a severe noise and vibration problem caused by wind flow. The vibration characteristics of the section were measured, and tests were carried out with two possible damping treatments.

One such treatment, infilling the structure with fine dry sand, was shown to be an effective damper in the critical frequency range. On-site tests were recommended to compare the effect of the wind on parapet sections with and without the sand infill.

The Summary contains 94 words. It, like the rest of the report, is put through the spell-check and also checked from a printout; the pages are then numbered. The title page is simple: it contains the title (**Vibration tests on Abiford Bridge**), Andrew's name and qualifications, the University name, the client's name and address and, of course, the date.

Andrew's Departmental Secretary has a supply of good quality cover sheets of the appropriate 'University colour', and he has taken care that the right information, title and author's name, appears through the 'window'. The secretary puts the whole report together into a spiral binding, and returns two copies to Andrew for final checking. He sends one to his clients and, with a feeling of a job well done, puts the other on his bookshelves.

The on-site tests were subsequently carried out, and Andrew's solution was accepted; he drives over the bridge with particular pleasure each day as he goes to work, and the people of Abiford sleep well.

References

1. The Institution of Electrical Engineers: *Technical Report Writing* (Professional Brief by Joan van Emden and Jennifer Easteal), 2nd edition, 1989

2. Buzan, Tony: *Use your head*, BBC Books, revised edition, 1982

3. Flanagan, Roger and Norman, George: *Life Cycle Costing for Construction*, Report published for the Royal Institution of Chartered Surveyors by Surveyors Publications, 1983

Bibliography

Booth, Vincent: *Communicating in Science: Writing and Speaking*, Cambridge University Press, 1985.

British Standards Institution: DD52: 1977 Draft for Development, *Recommendations for the Presentation of Tables, Graphs and Charts*, British Standards Institution, 1977.

Carey, G. V.: *Mind the Stop*, Penguin, 1971.

Gowers, Ernest: *The Complete Plain Words*, Pelican, revised 1987.

Haslam, J.: *Writing Engineering Specifications*, Spon, 1988.

Kirkman, John: *Good Style for Scientific and Engineering Writing*, Pitman, 1980.

Oxford English, Oxford University Press, 1986.

The Oxford Dictionary for Writers and Editors, Oxford University Press, 1990.

Turk, Christopher and Kirkman, John: *Effective Writing*, Spon, 1982.

van Emden, J.: *A Handbook of Writing for Engineers*, Macmillan, 1990.

Weiner, E. S. C.: *The Oxford Guide to English Usage*, Oxford University Press, 1983.